HELP!

D1584708

HELP!

Selections from *The Living Bible*

Compiled by Alice Hill
with additions by
Sheila Durrant

KINGSWAY PUBLICATIONS
EASTBOURNE

Selections from The Living Bible, © *1971, Tyndale House Publishers, Wheaton, Illinois.*

British Edition 1972
Reprinted 1973
New edition 1975
Reprinted 1977
Reprinted 1978

ISBN 0 902088 74 2

Printed in Great Britain for
KINGSWAY PUBLICATIONS LTD.,
Lottbridge Drove, Eastbourne, East Sussex BN23 6NT
by Hazell Watson & Viney Ltd, Aylesbury, Bucks

CONTENTS

ANGER

Psalm 103:8 He is merciful and tender towards those who don't deserve it: he is slow to get angry and full of kindness and love.

John 3:36 And all who trust him—God's Son—to save them have eternal life; those who don't believe and obey him shall never see heaven, but the wrath of God remains upon them.

Romans 1:18 But God shows his anger from heaven against all sinful, evil men who push away the truth from them.

Proverbs 15:1 A soft answer turns away wrath, but harsh words cause quarrels.

Proverbs 19:11 A wise man restrains his anger and overlooks insults.

Matthew 5:21, 22, 25a Under the law of Moses the rule was, "If you kill, you must die." But I have added to that rule, and tell you that if you are only ANGRY, even in your own home, you are in danger of judgment! If you call your friend an idiot, you are in danger of being brought before the court. And if you curse him you are in danger of the fires of hell . . . Come to terms quickly with your enemy before it is too late.

Ephesians 4:26, 27 If you are angry, don't sin by nursing your grudge. Don't let the sun go down with you still angry—get over it quickly; for when you are angry you give a mighty foothold to the devil.

Colossians 3:8, 13 Now is the time to cast off and throw away all these rotten garments of anger, hatred, cursing and dirty language . . . Be gentle and ready to forgive; never hold grudges.

ATTITUDES

1 Corinthians 16:14   And whatever you do, do it with kindness and love.

1 Thessalonians 5:18   Always be thankful no matter what happens, for that is God's will for you who belong to Christ Jesus.

2 Timothy 2:25, 26   Be humble when you are trying to teach those who are mixed up concerning the truth. For if you talk meekly and courteously to them they are more likely, with God's help, to turn away from their wrong ideas and believe what is true. Then they will come to their senses and escape from Satan's trap of slavery to sin which he uses to catch them whenever he likes, and then they can begin doing the will of God.

Hebrews 3:12   Beware of your own hearts . . . in case you should find that they too, are evil and unbelieving and are leading you away from the living God. Speak to each other about these things every day while there is still time, so that none of you will become hardened against God, being blinded by the glamour of sin.

Hebrews 13:17   Obey your spiritual leaders and be willing to do what they say. For their work is to watch over your souls, and God will judge them on how well they do this. Give them reason to report joyfully about you to the Lord and not with sorrow, for then you will suffer for it too.

1 Peter 4:8   Most important of all, continue to show deep love for each other, for love makes up for many of your faults.

1 Peter 4:14   Be happy if you are cursed and insulted for being a Christian, for when that happens the Spirit of God will come upon you with great glory.

2 Peter 1:6, 7   Learn to put aside your own desires so that you will become patient and godly, gladly letting God have his way with you.

This will make possible the next step, which is for you to enjoy other people and to like them, and finally you will grow to love them deeply.

1 John 2:9 Anyone who says he is walking in the light of Christ but hates his brother Christian is still in darkness.

Romans 12:9, 10, 11 Don't just pretend that you love others: really love them. Hate what is wrong. Stand on the side of the good.

Love each other with brotherly affection and take delight in honouring each other.

Never be lazy in your work but serve the Lord enthusiastically.

Proverbs 11:17 Your own soul is nourished when you are kind; it is destroyed when you are cruel.

Proverbs 15:33 Humility and reverence for the Lord will make you both wise and honoured.

Proverbs 16:18, 19 Pride goes before destruction and haughtiness before a fall. Better poor and humble than proud and rich.

Proverbs 17:22 A cheerful heart does good like medicine, but a broken spirit makes one sick.

Proverbs 18:12 Pride ends in destruction; humility ends in honour.

AUTHORITY

Ephesians 6:1–3 Children, obey your parents; this is the right thing to do because God has placed them in authority over you. Honour your father and mother. This is the first of God's Ten

Commandments that ends with a promise. And this is the promise: that if you honour your father and mother, yours will be a long life, full of blessing.

Romans 13:1, 2, 5 Obey the government, for God is the one who has put it there. There is no government anywhere that God has not placed in power. So those who refuse to obey the laws of the land are refusing to obey God, and punishment will follow.

Obey the laws, then, for two reasons: first, to keep from being punished, and second, just because you know you should.

BAD NEWS

Hebrews 4:13, 15 He knows about everyone, everywhere. Everything about us is bare and wide open to the all-seeing eyes of our living God; nothing can be hidden from him to whom we must explain all that we have done. This high priest of ours understands our weaknesses, since he had the same temptations we have, though he never once gave way to them and sinned.

1 Peter 5:7 Let him have all your worries and cares, for he is always thinking about you and watching everything that concerns you.

Isaiah 40:28–31 Don't you yet understand? Don't you know by now that the everlasting God, the Creator of the farthest parts of the earth, never grows faint or weary? No one can fathom the depths of his understanding. He gives power to the tired and worn out, and strength to the weak. Even the youths shall be exhausted, and the young men will all give up. But they that wait upon the Lord shall renew their strength. They shall mount up with wings like eagles; they shall run and not be weary; they shall walk and not faint.

BEHAVIOUR

1 Corinthians 16:14   And whatever you do, do it with kindness and love.

2 Corinthians 6:3, 4   We try to live in such a way that no one will ever be offended or kept back from finding the Lord by the way we act, so that no one can find fault with us and blame it on the Lord. In fact, in everything we do we try to show that we are true ministers of God. We patiently endure suffering and hardship and trouble of every kind.

2 Corinthians 13:5   Check up on yourselves. Are you really Christians? Do you pass the test? Do you feel Christ's presence and power more and more within you? Or are you just pretending to be Christians when actually you aren't at all?

1 Corinthians 5:11   . . . You are not to keep company with anyone who claims to be a brother Christian but indulges in sexual sins, or is greedy, or is a swindler, or worships idols, or is a drunkard, or abusive. Don't even eat a meal with such a person.

1 Corinthians 6:12   I can do anything I want to if Christ has not forbidden it, but some of these things aren't good for me. Even if I am allowed to do them, I'll refuse to if I think they might get such a grip on me that I can't easily stop when I want to.

1 Corinthians 10:24   Don't think only of yourself. Try to think of the other fellow, too, and what is best for him.

1 Corinthians 10:31–33   . . . It is because you must do everything for the glory of God, even your eating and drinking. So don't be a stumbling block to anyone . . . I try to please everyone in everything I do, not doing what I like or what is best for me but what is best for them, so that they may be saved.

13

Ephesians 5:15–17   So be careful how you act; these are difficult days. Don't be fools; be wise: make the most of every opportunity you have for doing good.

Don't act thoughtlessly, but try to find out and do whatever the Lord wants you to.

Galatians 6:4, 5, 7–10   Let everyone be sure that he is doing his very best, for then he will have the personal satisfaction of work well done, and won't need to compare himself with someone else. Each of us must bear some faults and burdens of his own. For none of us is perfect! Don't be misled; remember that you can't ignore God and get away with it: a man will always reap just the kind of crop he sows!

If he sows to please his own wrong desires, he will be planting seeds of evil and he will surely reap a harvest of spiritual decay and death; but if he plants the good things of the spirit, he will reap the everlasting life which the Holy Spirit gives him.

And let us not get tired of doing what is right, for after a while we will reap a harvest of blessing if we don't get discouraged and give up. That's why whenever we can we should always be kind to everyone, and especially to our Christian brothers.

Philippians 2:3, 5   Don't be selfish; don't live to make a good impression on others. Be humble, thinking of others as better than yourself. Your attitude should be the kind that was shown us by Jesus Christ. . . .

Colossians 3:5–10   Away then with sinful, earthly things; deaden the evil desires lurking within you; have nothing to do with sexual sin, impurity, lust, and shameful desires; don't worship the good things of this life, for that is idolatry. God's terrible anger is upon those who do such things. You used to do them when your life was still part of this world; but now is the time to cast off and throw away all these rotten garments of anger, hatred, cursing, and dirty language. Don't tell lies to each other; it was your old life with all its wickedness that did that sort of thing; now it is dead and gone. You are living a brand new kind of life that is continually learning more and more of what is right, and trying constantly to be more and more like Christ who created this new life within you.

1 Timothy 1:19   Cling tightly to your faith in Christ and always keep your conscience clear, doing what you know is right. For some people have disobeyed their consciences and have deliberately done what they knew was wrong. It isn't surprising that soon they lost their faith in Christ after defying God like that.

1 Timothy 4:12   Don't let anyone think little of you because you are young. Be their ideal; let them follow the way you teach and live; be a pattern for them in your love, your faith, and your clean thoughts.

Hebrews 12:13   . . . And mark out a straight, smooth path for your feet so that those who follow you, though weak and lame, will not fall and hurt themselves, but become strong.

James 3:8, 9   . . . But no human being can tame the tongue. It is always ready to pour out its deadly poison. Sometimes it praises our heavenly Father, and sometimes it breaks out into curses against men who are made like God.

1 Peter 1:14   Obey God because you are his children; don't slip back into your old ways—doing evil because you knew no better.

1 Peter 4:3–5   You have had enough in the past of the evil things the godless enjoy—sexual sin, lust, getting drunk, wild parties, drinking bouts, and the worship of idols—which leads to other terrible sins. Of course, your former friends will be very surprised when you don't eagerly join them any more in the wicked things they do, and they will laugh at you in contempt and scorn. But just remember that they must face the Judge of all, living and dead; they will be punished for the way they have lived.

1 John 3:18 . . . Let us stop just saying we love people; let us really love them, and show it by our actions.

1 John 3:6, 7 So if we stay close to him, obedient to him, we won't be sinning either. . . . If you are constantly doing what is good it is because you *are* good, even as he is.

Proverbs 10:14 A wise man holds his tongue. Only a fool blurts out everything he knows; that only leads to sorrow and trouble.

Proverbs 10:19 Don't talk so much. Every time you open your mouth you put your foot in it. Be sensible and turn off the flow!

Proverbs 11:12, 13 To quarrel with a neighbour is foolish; a man with good sense holds his tongue. A gossip goes around spreading rumours, while a trustworthy man tries to quiet them.

Proverbs 12:16 A fool is quick-tempered; a wise man stays cool when insulted.

Proverbs 18:1, 2 The selfish man quarrels against every sound principle of conduct by demanding his own way. A rebel doesn't care about the facts. All he wants to do is yell.

Proverbs 20:1 Wine gives false courage; hard liquor leads to brawls; what fools men are to let it master them, making them reel drunkenly down the street!

Proverbs 15:1 A soft answer turns away wrath, but harsh words cause quarrels.

Proverbs 15:4 Gentle words cause life and health; grumbling brings discouragement.

Proverbs 20:19 Don't tell your secrets to a gossip unless you want them broadcast to the world.

Proverbs 21:8 A man is known by his actions. An evil man lives an evil life; a good man lives a godly life.

Proverbs 24:21, 22   My son, watch your step before the Lord and the king, and don't associate with radicals. For you will go down with them to sudden disaster, and who knows where it all will end?

Proverbs 28:13   A man who refuses to admit his mistakes can never be successful. But if he confesses and forsakes them, he gets another chance.

Proverbs 29:22   A hot-tempered man starts fights and gets into all kinds of trouble.

THE BIBLE

2 Timothy 3:16, 17   Every Scripture was given to us by inspiration from God and is invaluable to teach us what is true and to make us realize what is wrong in our lives; it straightens us out and helps us do what is right. It is God's way of making us well prepared at every point, fully equipped to do good to everyone.

Hebrews 4:12   For whatever God says to us is full of living power: it is sharper than the sharpest dagger, cutting swift and deep into every aspect of our innermost thoughts and desires, exposing us for what we really are.

Psalm 119:9, 11, 16, 24, 96, 97, 98, 105   How can a young man stay pure? By reading your Word and following its rules.
   I have thought much about your words, and stored them in my heart so that they would hold me back from sin.
   I will delight in them and not forget them.
   Your laws are both my light and my counsellors.
   Nothing is perfect except your words. Oh, how I love them. I think about them all day long. They make me wiser than my enemies, because they are my constant guide. Your words are

a flashlight to light the path ahead of me, and keep me from stumbling.

Matthew 22:29   But Jesus said, "Your error is caused by your ignorance of the Scriptures and of God's power."

Matthew 7:24   All who listen to my instructions and follow them are wise, like a man who builds his house on solid rock.

Mark 13:31   Heaven and earth shall disappear, but my words stand sure for ever.

Romans 10:17   Yet faith comes from listening to this Good News—the Good News about Christ.

Colossians 3:16   Remember what Christ taught and let his words enrich your lives and make you wise; teach them to each other and sing them out in psalms and hymns and spiritual songs, singing to the Lord with thankful hearts.

Isaiah 40:8   The grass withers, the flowers fade, but the Word of our God shall stand forever.

Proverbs 13:13   Despise God's Word and find yourself in trouble. Obey it and succeed.

BLOW YOUR MIND!

Hebrews 13:5b   For God has said, "I will never, never fail you nor forsake you."

James 1:17   But whatever is good and perfect comes to us from God, the creator of all light, and he shines for ever without change or shadow.

James 4:8a   When you draw close to God, God will draw close to you.

1 Peter 2:19, 20 Praise the Lord if you are punished for doing right! . . . if you do right and suffer for it, and are patient beneath the blows, God is well pleased.

Titus 3:1 . . . Obey the government and its officers and always be obedient and ready for any honest work.

1 Peter 2:13 For the Lord's sake obey every law of your government. . . .

Romans 13:1–3, 5 Obey the government, for God is the one who has put it there. There is no government anywhere that God has not placed in power. So those who refuse to obey the laws of the land are refusing to obey God, and punishment will follow. For the magistrate does not frighten people who are doing right; but those doing evil will always fear him. So if you don't want to be afraid, keep the laws and you will get along well. Obey the laws, then, for two reasons: first, to keep from being punished, and second, just because you know you should.

BODY

1 Corinthians 6:15–20 Don't you realize that your bodies are actually parts and members of Christ? So should I take part of Christ and join him to a prostitute? Never! And don't you know that if a man joins himself to a prostitute she becomes a part of him and he becomes a part of her? For God tells us in the Scripture that in his sight the two become one person. But if you give yourself to the Lord, you and Christ are joined together as one person.

That is why I say you should steer clear of sexual immorality. When you sin in this way it is against your own body. Haven't you yet learned that your body is the home of the Holy Spirit God gave you, and that he lives within you? Your own body does not belong to you. For God has bought you with a great price. So use every part of your body to give glory back to God, because he owns it.

1 Corinthians 9:27a   Like an athlete I punish my body, treating it roughly, training it to do what it should, not what it wants to.

Romans 12:1   . . . I plead with you to give your bodies to God. Let them be a living sacrifice, holy—the kind he can accept. When you think of what he has done for you, is this too much to ask?

Proverbs 15:13   A happy face means a glad heart; a sad face means a breaking heart.

Proverbs 16:27   Idle hands are the devil's workshop; idle lips are his mouthpiece.

Proverbs 17:22   A cheerful heart does good like medicine, but a broken spirit makes one sick.

Proverbs 18:14   A man's courage can sustain his broken body, but when courage dies, what hope is left?

Proverbs 20:12   If you have good eyesight and good hearing, thank God who gave them to you.

Matthew 6:22, 23, 25   If your eye is pure, there will be sunshine in your soul. But if your eye is clouded with evil thoughts and desires, you are in deep spiritual darkness. And oh, how deep that darkness can be!
So my counsel is: Don't worry about things—food, drink, money and clothes. For you already have life and a body—and they are far more important than what to eat and wear.

Luke 11:34–36   Your eye lights up your inward being. A pure eye lets sunshine into your soul. A lustful eye shuts out the light and plunges you into darkness. So watch out that the sunshine isn't blotted out. If you are filled with light within, with no dark corners, then the outside will be radiant too, as though a floodlight is beamed upon you.

CHURCH

Matthew 16:18   You are Peter, a stone; and upon this rock I will build my church; and all the powers of hell shall not prevail against it.

Ephesians 5:25b–27   . . . the same kind of love . . . as Christ showed to the church when he died for her, to make her holy and clean, washed by baptism and God's word; so that he could give her to himself as a glorious church without a single spot or wrinkle or any other blemish, being holy and without a single fault.

Colossians 1:18   He (Christ) is the head of the body made up of his people—that is, his church—which he began . . .

Acts 2:42, 44, 47   They joined with the other believers in regular attendance at the apostles' teaching sessions and at the breaking of bread services and in prayer. . . . and all the believers met together constantly and shared everything with each other . . . and each day God added to them all who were being saved.

Ephesians 2:19   Now you are no longer strangers to God and foreigners to heaven, but you are members of God's very own family, citizens of God's country, and you belong in God's household with every other Christian.

1 Corinthians 12:12, 22, 27   Our bodies have many parts, but the many parts make up only one body when they are all put together. So it is with the "body" of Christ. Each of us is a part of the one body of Christ . . . and some of the parts that seem weakest and least important are really the most necessary . . . all of you together are the one body of Christ and each one of you is a separate and necessary part of it.

Romans 12:4, 5   Just as there are many parts to our bodies, so it is with Christ's body. We are all parts of it, and it takes every one of us to make it complete, for we each have different work to do. So we belong to each other, and each needs all the others.

Hebrews 10:25 Let us not neglect our church duties and meetings, as some people do, but encourage and warn each other, especially now that the day of his coming back again is drawing near.

DEATH

1 Corinthians 15:22 Everyone dies because all of us are related to Adam, being members of his sinful race, and wherever there is sin, death results. But all who are related to Christ will rise again.

2 Corinthians 5:1 For we know that when this tent we live in now is taken down—when we die and leave these bodies—we will have wonderful new bodies in heaven, homes that will be ours for evermore, made for us by God himself, and not by human hands.

John 11:25, 26 I am the one who raises the dead and gives them life again. Anyone who believes in me, even though he dies like anyone else, shall live again. He is given eternal life for believing in me and shall never perish.

DECISIONS

Proverbs 18:13 What a shame—yes, how stupid!—to decide before knowing the facts!

Proverbs 16:1 We can make our plans, but the final outcome is in God's hands.

Proverbs 19:2, 3   It is dangerous and sinful to rush into the unknown. A man may ruin his chances by his own foolishness and then blame it on the Lord!

DIRECTION FROM GOD

James 1:5, 6   If you want to know what God wants you to do, ask him, and he will gladly tell you, for he is always ready to give a generous supply of wisdom to all who ask him; he will not resent it. But when you ask him, be sure that you really expect him to tell you, for a doubtful mind will be as unsettled as a wave of the sea that is driven and tossed by the wind; and every decision you then make will be uncertain, as you turn first this way, and then that. If you don't ask with faith don't expect the Lord to give you any solid answer.

James 4:2b, 3   And yet the reason you don't have what you want is that you don't ask God for it. And even when you do ask you don't get it because your whole aim is wrong—you want only what will give *you* pleasure.

Proverbs 3:5, 6   . . . Trust the Lord completely; don't ever trust yourself. In everything you do, put God first, and he will direct you and crown your efforts with success.

Psalm 37:23, 24   The steps of good men are directed by the Lord; He delights in each step they take. If they fall it isn't fatal, for the Lord holds them with his hand.

Psalm 25:4, 5, 8, 9   Show me the path where I should go, O Lord; point out the right road for me to walk. Lead me; teach me; for you are the God who gives me salvation. I have no hope except in you.
  The Lord is good and glad to teach the proper path to all who go astray; he will teach the ways that are right and best to

those who humbly turn to him. And when we obey him, every path he guides us on is fragrant with his lovingkindness and his truth.

Proverbs 20:24   Since the Lord is directing our steps, why try to understand everything that happens along the way?

Psalm 37:5   Commit everything you do to the Lord. Trust him to help you do it and he will.

Psalm 37:34a   Don't be impatient for the Lord to act!

DISCIPLINE

Hebrews 12:5–8, 11   And have you quite forgotten the encouraging words God spoke to you, his child? He said, ''My son, don't be angry when the Lord punishes you. Don't be discouraged when he has to show you where you are wrong. For when he punishes you, it proves that he loves you. When he whips you it proves you are really his child.

Let God train you, for he is doing what any loving father does for his children. Whoever heard of a son who was never corrected? If God doesn't punish you when you need it, as other fathers punish their sons, then it means that you aren't really God's son at all—that you don't really belong in his family.

Being punished isn't enjoyable while it is happening—it hurts! But afterwards we can see the result, a quiet growth in grace and character.

Psalm 119:75, 76, 77   I know, O Lord, that your decisions are right and that your punishment was right and did me good. Now let your lovingkindness comfort me, just as you promised. Surround me with your tender mercies, that I may live. For your law is my delight.

Proverbs 3:11, 12   Young man, do not resent it when God chastens and corrects you, for his punishment is proof of his love. Just as a father punishes a son he delights in to make him better, so the Lord corrects you.

Proverbs 13:24   If you refuse to discipline your son, it proves you don't love him; for if you love him you will be prompt to punish him.

Proverbs 20:30   Punishment that hurts chases evil from the heart.

Proverbs 29:15, 17, 19   Scolding and spanking a child helps him to learn. Left to himself, he brings shame to his mother.
   Discipline your son and he will give you happiness and peace of mind.
   Sometimes mere words are not enough—discipline is needed. For the words may not be heeded.

Proverbs 19:18   Discipline your son in his early years while there is hope. If you don't you will ruin his life.

DOUBT

Jeremiah 14:5   The Lord said to me, "I knew you before you were formed within your mother's womb."

Job 38:1, 2, 42:5   Then the Lord answered Job from the whirlwind: "Why are you using your ignorance to deny my providence?"
Read from here to the beginning of chapter *42* . . . (Job said,) "I have heard about you before, but now I have seen you, and I loathe myself and repent in dust and ashes."

Psalm 139:7–11   I can never be lost to your Spirit! I can never get away from my God! If I go up to heaven, you are there; if I go down to the place of the dead, you are there. If I ride the morning winds to the farthest ocean, even there your hand will guide me, your strength will support me. If I try to hide in the darkness, the night becomes light around me.

Matthew 21:21, 22   Then Jesus told them, "Truly, if you have faith, and don't doubt, you can do things like this and much more . . . you can get anything—ANYTHING you ask for in prayer—if you believe."

Mark 9:23, 24   . . . "Anything is possible if you have faith." The father instantly replied, "I *do* have faith; oh, help me to have *more*!"

John 20:27–29   Then he said to Thomas, "Put your finger into my hands. Put your hand into my side. Don't be faithless any longer. Believe!" "My Lord and my God!" Thomas said. Then Jesus told him, "You believe because you have seen me. But blessed are those who haven't seen me and believe anyway."

James 1:6, 8   . . . a doubtful mind will be as unsettled as a wave of the sea that is driven and tossed by the wind . . . If you don't ask with faith, don't expect the Lord to give you any solid answer.

Hebrews 13:8   Jesus Christ is the same yesterday, today and forever.

ENVY

Exodus 20:17   You must not be envious of your neighbour's house, or want to sleep with his wife, or want to own his slaves, oxen, donkeys, or anything else he has.

Proverbs 24:19, 20   Don't envy the wicked. Don't covet his riches. For the evil man has no future, his light will be snuffed out.

Matthew 6:31–33 Don't worry at all about having enough food and clothing. Why be like the heathen? For they take pride in all these things and are deeply concerned about them. But your heavenly Father already knows perfectly well that you need them. And he will gladly give them to you if you give him first place in your life.

Hebrews 13:5 Stay away from the love of money; be satisfied with what you have. For God has said, "I will never, *never* fail you nor forsake you."

Philippians 4:12 I know how to live on almost nothing or with everything. I have learned the secret of contentment in every situation, whether it be a full stomach or hunger, plenty or want.

Psalm 17:15 My contentment is not in wealth but in seeing you and knowing all is well between us. And when I awake in heaven, I will be fully satisfied, for I will see you face to face.

1 Corinthians 13:4 Love is very patient and kind, never jealous or envious, never boastful or proud, never haughty or selfish or rude.

Galatians 5:19–22 When you follow your own wrong inclinations, your lives will produce these evil results . . . jealousy and anger . . . envy, murder . . . But when the Holy Spirit controls our lives, he will produce this kind of fruit in us: love, joy, peace . . .

FAITH

Hebrews 11:1 What is faith? It is the confident assurance that something we want is going to happen. It is the certainty that what we hope for is waiting for us, even though we cannot see it ahead.

Hebrews 11:6 You can never please God without faith, without depending on him. Anyone who wants to come to God must believe that there is a God and that he rewards those who sincerely look for him.

Read all of Hebrews *11*.

James 2:17b Faith that doesn't show itself by good works is no faith at all—it is dead and useless.

Romans 10:17 Yet faith comes from listening to this Good News—the Good News about Christ.

Matthew 21:22 You can get anything—anything you ask for in prayer—if you believe.

Mark 9:23 . . . Anything is possible if you have faith.

FALSE TEACHERS

1 John 4:1, 2 Dearly loved friends, don't always believe everything you hear just because someone says it is a message from God: test it first to see if it really is. For there are many false teachers around, and the way to find out if their message is from the Holy Spirit is to ask: Does it really agree that Jesus Christ, God's Son, actually became man with a human body? If so, then the message is from God.

2 John 1:7, 9–11 Watch out for the false leaders—and there are many of them around—who don't believe that Jesus Christ came to earth as a human being with a body like ours. Such people are against the truth and against Christ.

For if you wander beyond the teaching of Christ, you will leave God behind; while if you are loyal to Christ's teachings, you will have God too. Then you will have both the Father and the Son.

If anyone comes to teach you, and he doesn't believe what

Christ taught, don't even invite him into your home. Don't encourage him in any way.

If you do you will be a partner with him in his wickedness.

Proverbs 19:27   Stop listening to teaching that contradicts what you know is right.

Matthew 7:15–21   Beware of false teachers who come disguised as harmless sheep, but are wolves and will tear you apart. You can detect them by the way they act, just as you can identify a tree by its fruit. You need never confuse grapevines with thorn bushes or figs with thistles. Different kinds of fruit trees can quickly be identified by examining their fruit. A variety that produces delicious fruit never produces an inedible kind. And a tree producing an inedible kind can't produce what is good. So the trees having the inedible fruit are chopped down and thrown on the fire. Yes, the way to identify a tree or a person is by the kind of fruit produced. Not all who talk like godly people are godly. They may refer to me as "Lord", but still won't get to heaven. For the decisive question is whether they obey my Father in heaven.

Jude 1:4, 13b   . . . Some godless teachers have wormed their way in among you, saying that after we become Christians we can do just as we like without fear of God's punishment. The fate of such people was written long ago, for they have turned against our only Master and Lord, Jesus Christ. . . . Ahead of them is the everlasting gloom and darkness that God has prepared for them.

FAMILY LIFE

Proverbs 6:20–23   Young man, obey your father and your mother. Tie their instructions around your finger so you won't forget. Take to heart all of their advice. Every day and all night long their counsel will lead you and save you from harm; when you wake up in the morning, let their instructions guide you into the new day. For their advice is a beam of light directed into the dark corners of your mind to warn you of danger and to give you a good life.

Proverbs 17:1 A dry crust eaten in peace is better than steak every day along with argument and strife.

Proverbs 19:13, 18, 26 A rebellious son is a calamity to his father. . . .

Discipline your son in his early years while there is hope. If you don't you will ruin his life.

A son who mistreats his father or mother is a public disgrace.

Proverbs 20:7 It is a wonderful heritage to have an honest father.

Proverbs 15:5 Only a fool despises his father's advice; a wise son considers each suggestion.

Proverbs 29:15, 17, 19 Scolding and spanking a child helps him to learn. Left to himself, he brings shame to his mother.

Discipline your son and he will give you happiness and peace of mind.

Sometimes mere words are not enough—discipline is needed. For the words may not be heeded.

Proverbs 30:11–14 There are those who curse their father and mother, and feel themselves faultless despite their many sins. They are proud beyond description, arrogant, disdainful. They devour the poor with teeth as sharp as knives!

Proverbs 22:6 Teach a child to choose the right path, and when he is older he will remain upon it.

Psalm 101:2 I will try to walk a blameless path, but how I need your help, especially in my own home, where I long to act as I should.

Psalm 133:1 How wonderful it is, how pleasant, when brothers live in harmony!

FEAR

Proverbs 9:10   For the reverence and fear of God are basic to all wisdom.

Psalm 23:4   Even when walking through the dark valley of death I will not be afraid, for you are close beside me, guarding, guiding all the way.

Psalm 27:1   The Lord is my light and my salvation; whom shall I fear?

Proverbs 29:25   Fear of man is a dangerous trap, but to trust in God means safety.

Isaiah 41:10   Fear not, for I am with you. Do not be dismayed. I am your God. I will strengthen you; I will help you; I will uphold you with my victorious right hand.

Romans 8:15   And so we should not be like cringing, fearful slaves, but we should behave like God's very own children, adopted into the bosom of his family, and calling to him, "Father, Father."

Hebrews 13:5b, 6   For God has said, "I will never, NEVER fail you nor forsake you." That is why we can say without any doubt or fear, "The Lord is my helper and I am not afraid of anything that mere man can do to me."

1 John 4:18   We need have no fear of someone who loves us perfectly; his perfect love for us eliminates all dread of what he might do to us. If we are afraid, it is for fear of what he might do to us, and shows that we are not fully convinced that he really loves us.

Luke 21:26, 28   The courage of many people will falter because of the fearful fate they see coming upon the earth . . . when all these things begin to happen, stand straight and look up! For your salvation is near.

FORGIVENESS

2 Corinthians 5:19 For God was in Christ, restoring the world to himself, no longer counting men's sins against them but blotting them out. This is the wonderful message he has given us to tell others.

Ephesians 4:32 Be kind to each other, tenderhearted, forgiving one another, just as God has forgiven you because you belong to Christ.

Matthew 18:21, 22 Then Peter came to him and asked, "Sir, how often should I forgive a brother who sins against me? Seven times?"

"No!" Jesus replied, "seventy times seven!"

FREEDOM

Galatians 5:1a So Christ has made us free.

Galatians 5:13 ... You have been given freedom: not freedom to do wrong, but freedom to love and serve each other.

John 8:32 ... You will know the truth and the truth will set you free.

1 Corinthians 6:12 I can do anything I want to if Christ has not forbidden it, but some of these things aren't good for me.

FRIENDSHIP

Proverbs 17:17 A true friend is always loyal, and a brother is born to help in time of need.

Proverbs 18:19 It is harder to win back the friendship of an offended brother than to capture a fortified city. His anger shuts you out like iron bars.

Proverbs 18:24 There are "friends" who pretend to be friends, but there is a friend who sticks closer than a brother.

Proverbs 27:10 Never abandon a friend—either yours or your father's. Then you won't need to go to a distant relative for help in your time of need.

Matthew 5:23, 24 So if you are standing before the altar in the Temple, offering a sacrifice to God, and suddenly remember that a friend has something against you, leave your sacrifice there beside the altar and go and apologize and be reconciled to him, and then come and offer your sacrifice to God.

FRUSTRATION

Job 3:23 Why is man allowed to be born if God is only going to give him a hopeless life of uselessness and frustration?

Psalm 32:3, 5 There was a time when I wouldn't admit what a sinner I was. But my dishonesty made me miserable and filled my days with frustration . . . I finally admitted all my sins to you and stopped trying to hide them. I said to myself, "I will confess them to the Lord." And you forgave me! All my guilt is gone.

Proverbs 27:3 A rebel's frustrations are heavier than sand and rocks.

Psalm 37:4, 5 Be delighted with the Lord. Then he will give you all your heart's desires. Commit everything you do to the Lord. Trust him to help you do it and he will.

Philippians 3:11 So, whatever it takes, I will be one who

33

lives in the newness of life of those who are alive from the dead.

1 Timothy 1:3b   He is my father's God, and mine, and my only purpose in life is to please him.

Hebrews 12:1b   . . . let us run with patience the particular race that God has set before us.

Galatians 6:9   And let us not get tired of doing what is right, for after a while we will reap a harvest of blessing if we don't get discouraged and give up.

GOD

Psalm 11:4   But the Lord is still in his holy temple: he still rules from heaven. He closely watches everything that happens here on earth.

Psalm 18:30   What a God he is! How perfect in every way! All his promises prove true. He is a shield for everyone who hides behind him.

Psalm 46:1   God is our refuge and strength, a tested help in times of trouble.

Psalm 100:5   For the Lord is always good. He is always loving and kind, and his faithfulness goes on and on to each succeeding generation.

Psalm 147:5   How great he is! His power is absolute! His understanding is unlimited.

Proverbs 21:30   No one, regardless of how shrewd or well-advised he is, can stand against the Lord.

Psalm 89:8b   Faithfulness is your very character.

Acts 17:24–28   He made the world and everything in it, and since he is Lord of heaven and earth, he doesn't live in man-made temples; and human hands can't minister to his needs—for he has no needs! He himself gives life and breath to everything, and satisfies every need there is. He created all the people of the world from one common source, and scattered the nations across the face of the earth. He decided beforehand which should rise and fall, and when. He determined their boundaries.

His purpose in all of this is that they should seek after God, and perhaps feel their way towards him and find him—though he is not far from any one of us. For in him we live and move and exist. As one of your own poets puts it, "We are the sons of God."

Psalm 103:1, 5a, 8–10, 12, 13   I bless the holy name of God with all my heart.

He fills my life with good things!

He is merciful and tender towards those who don't deserve it; he is slow to get angry and full of kindness and love! He has not punished us as we deserve for all our sins.

He has removed our sins as far away from us as the east is from the west. He is like a father to us, tender and sympathetic to those who reverence him.

Numbers 23:19   God is not a man, that he should lie; he doesn't change his mind like humans do. Has he ever promised, without doing what he said?

GOD'S DAY

Genesis 2:2, 3   So on the seventh day, having finished his task, God ceased from this work he had been doing, and God blessed the seventh day and declared it holy, because it was the day when he ceased this work of creation.

Exodus 20:8–11 Remember to observe the Sabbath as a holy day. Six days a week are for your daily duties and your regular work, but the seventh day is a day of Sabbath rest before the Lord your God. On that day you are to do no work of any kind, nor shall your son, daughter, or slaves—whether men or women—or your cattle or your house guests. For in six days the Lord made the heaven, earth and sea, and everything in them, and rested the seventh day; so he blessed the Sabbath day and set it aside for rest.

Isaiah 58:13, 14 If you keep the Sabbath holy, not having your own fun and business on that day, but enjoying the Sabbath and speaking of it with delight as the Lord's holy day, and honouring the Lord in what you do, not following your own desires and pleasure, nor talking idly—then the Lord will be your delight . . .

Matthew 12:10b, 12b "Is it legal to work by healing on the Sabbath?" . . .
  "Yes, it is right to do good on the Sabbath."

Mark 2:27 But the Sabbath was made to benefit man, and not man to benefit the Sabbath.

John 4:22 . . . it's not *where* we worship that counts, but how we worship—is our worship spiritual and real? For God is Spirit, and we must have his help to worship as we should.

Romans 14:6 If you have special days for worshipping the Lord, you are trying to honour him; you are doing a good thing.

Revelation 1:10 It was the Lord's Day and I was worshipping . . .

GOD'S PURPOSE FOR OUR LIVES

Psalm 18:30a As for God, his way is perfect.

Ephesians 1:5, 7, 9–13 His unchanging plan has always been to adopt us into his own family by sending Jesus Christ to die for us. And he did this because he wanted to.

So overflowing is his kindness towards us that he took away all our sins through the blood of his Son, by whom we are saved.

God has told us his secret reason for sending Christ, a plan he decided on in mercy long ago . . . that when the time is ripe he will gather us all together from wherever we are—in heaven or on earth—to be with him in Christ, for ever.

Because of what Christ has done we have become gifts to God that he delights in, for as part of God's sovereign plan we were chosen from the beginning to be his, and all things happen just as he decided long ago. God's purpose in this was that we should praise God and give glory to him for doing these mighty things for us, who were the first to trust in Christ.

And because of what Christ did, all you others too, who heard the Good News about how to be saved, and trusted Christ, were marked as belonging to Christ by the Holy Spirit, who long ago had been promised to all of us Christians.

Romans 8:28, 29 And we know that all that happens to us is working for our good if we love God and are fitting into his plans. For from the very beginning God decided that those who came to him—and all along he knew who would—should become like his Son, so that his Son would be the firstborn, with many brothers.

GOD'S WORK

1 Corinthians 7:30 . . . Happiness or sadness or wealth should not keep anyone from doing God's work.

Luke 9:62 But Jesus told him, "Anyone who lets himself be distracted from the work I plan for him is not fit for the Kingdom of God."

Acts 20:24 But life is worth nothing unless I use it for doing the work assigned me by the Lord Jesus—the work of telling others the Good News about God's mighty kindness and love.

GRACE

Romans 3:23, 24 Yes, all have sinned; all fall short of God's glorious ideal; yet now God declares us "not guilty" of offending him if we trust in Jesus Christ, who in his kindness freely takes away our sins.

Romans 5:20b . . . the more we see our sinfulness, the more we see God's abounding grace forgiving us.

Romans 6:15b, 23 . . . our salvation does not depend on keeping the law, but on receiving God's grace . . . for the wages of sin is death, but the free gift of God is eternal life through Jesus Christ our Lord.

2 Corinthians 8:9 You know how full of love and kindness our Lord Jesus was: though he was so very rich, yet to help you he became so very poor . . .

Ephesians 1:3 How we praise God, the Father of our Lord Jesus Christ, who has blessed us with every blessing in heaven because we belong to Christ.

Ephesians 2:4–9   But God is so rich in mercy; he loved us so much that even though we were spiritually dead and doomed by our sins, he gave us back our lives again when he raised Christ from the dead—only by his undeserved favour have we ever been saved—and lifted us up from the grave into glory along with Christ, where we sit with him in the heavenly realms—all because of what Christ Jesus did. And now God can always point to us as examples of how very, very rich his kindness is, as shown in all he has done for us through Jesus Christ. Because of his kindness you have been saved through trusting Christ. And even trusting is not of yourselves; it too is a gift from God. Salvation is not a reward for the good we have done, so none of us can take any credit for it.

GUILT

Genesis 3:11–12   "Who told you you were naked?" the Lord God asked. "Have you eaten fruit from the tree I warned you about?" "Yes," Adam admitted.

Psalm 51:3, 5, 12, 13   . . . I admit my shameful deed —it haunts me day and night . . . But I was born a sinner, yes, from the moment my mother conceived me. Restore to me again the joy of your salvation, and make me willing to obey you. Then I will teach your ways to other sinners, and they—guilty like me—will repent and return to you.

James 2:10   And the person who keeps every law of God, but makes one little slip, is just as guilty as the person who has broken every law there is.

1 John 1:8, 9a   If we say that we have no sin, we are only fooling ourselves, and refusing to accept the truth. But if we confess our sins to him, he can be depended on to forgive us and to cleanse us from every wrong.

Isaiah 53:66   God laid on him the guilt and sins of every one of us.

Romans 3:23, 24   Yes, all have sinned; all fall short of God's glorious ideal; yet now God declares us "not guilty" of offending him if we trust in Jesus Christ, who in his kindness freely takes away our sins.

Romans 8:1   So there is now no condemnation awaiting those who belong to Christ Jesus.

1 John 3:20, 21   . . . If we have bad consciences and feel that we have done wrong, the Lord will feel it even more acutely, for he knows everything we do. But . . . if our consciences are clear, we can come to the Lord with perfect assurance and trust.

HEAVEN

Psalm 17:15b   . . . when I awake in heaven, I will be fully satisfied, for I will see you face to face.

Matthew 7:13a, 21   Heaven can be entered only through the narrow gate . . . not all who talk like godly people are godly. They may refer to me as 'Lord', but still won't get to heaven. For the decisive question is whether they obey my Father, in heaven.

Read the whole of Matthew chapter *13* on the Kingdom of Heaven.

Luke 20:34, 35   . . . marriage is for people here on earth, but when those who are counted worthy of being raised from the dead get to heaven, they do not marry. And they never die again. In these respects they are like angels, and are sons of God, for they are raised up in a new life from the dead.

1 Corinthians 15:51, 53   . . . we shall not all die, but we shall all be given new bodies! For our earthly bodies, the ones we have now that can die, must be transformed into heavenly bodies that cannot perish but will live for ever.

2 Corinthians 5:1, 3 . . . wonderful new bodies . . . homes that will be ours for evermore, made for us by God himself, and not by human hands . . . for we shall not be merely spirits without bodies.

Colossians 3:3b . . . Your real life is in heaven with Christ and God.

HELL

Revelation 1:13, 17, 18 And standing among them was one who looked like Jesus who called himself the Son of Man . . . he laid his right hand on me and said, "Don't be afraid! I am the first and last, the living one who died, who is now alive for evermore, who has the keys of hell and death—don't be afraid!"

Matthew 13:40–42 . . . so shall it be at the end of the world: I will send my angels and they will separate out of the Kingdom every temptation and all who are evil, and throw them into the furnace and burn them. There shall be weeping and gnashing of teeth.

Matthew 25:41, 46 "Then I will turn to those on my left and say, 'Away with you, you cursed ones, into the eternal fire prepared for the devil and his demons'. . . . and they will go away into eternal punishment; but the righteous will go into everlasting life."

Luke 16:19–31 Story of Dives and Lazarus, especially verse *31*.

John 3:16–19 For God loved the world so much that he gave his only Son so that anyone who believes in him shall not perish but have eternal life. God did not send his Son into the world to condemn it, but to save it. There is no eternal doom awaiting those who trust him to save them. But those who don't trust him have already been tried and condemned for not believing in the only Son of God. Their sentence is based on this fact: that the light from heaven came into the world, but they loved the darkness more than the light, for their deeds were evil.

Revelation 20:14, 15   And death and hell were thrown into the lake of fire. This is the second death—the lake of fire. And if anyone's name was not found recorded in the Book of Life, he was thrown into the lake of fire.

2 Thessalonians 1:9b   . . . forever separated from the face of the Lord, never to see the glory of his power.

2 Timothy 4:8   . . . the Lord, the righteous Judge . . .

HOLINESS

Exodus 15:11   Who else is like the Lord among the gods? Who is glorious in holiness like him? Who is so awesome in splendour, a wonder-working God?

Isaiah 6:36   Holy, holy, holy is the Lord of heaven's armies; the whole earth is filled with his glory.

Psalm 96:9a   Worship the Lord with the beauty of holy lives.

John 17:17–19   "(Father) make them pure and holy through teaching them your words of truth. As you sent me into the world, I am sending them into the world. And I consecrate myself to meet their need for growth in truth and holiness."

Romans 12:1   . . . I plead with you to give your bodies to God. Let them be a living sacrifice, holy—the kind he can accept. When you think of what he has done for you, is this too much to ask?

1 Corinthians 3:16–17 Don't you realize that all of you to-gether are the house of God, and that the Spirit of God lives among you in this house? If anyone defiles and spoils God's house, God will destroy him. For God's home is holy and clean, and you are that home.

Ephesians 1:4 Long ago, even before he made the world, God chose us to be his very own, through what Christ would do for us; he decided then to make us holy in his eyes, without a single fault—we who stand before him covered with his love.

Hebrews 10:14 By that one offering (Christ), he made for ever perfect in the sight of God all those whom he is making holy.

1 Peter 1:14–16 Obey God because you are his children; don't slip back into your old ways—doing evil because you knew no better. But be holy now in everything you do, just as the Lord is holy, who invited you to be his child. He himself has said, "You must be holy, for I am holy."

THE HOLY SPIRIT

1 Corinthians 2:10, 12 But we know about these things be-cause God has sent his Spirit to tell us, and his Spirit searches out and shows us all of God's deepest secrets.

And God has actually given us his Spirit (not the world's spirit) to tell us about the wonderful free gifts of grace and blessing that God has given us.

1 Corinthians 2:14 . . . only those who have the Holy Spirit within them can understand what the Holy Spirit means.

1 Corinthians 12:7, 13b The Holy Spirit displays God's power through each of us as a means of helping the entire church.

The Holy Spirit has fitted us all together into one body.

Galatians 5:22, 23, 25, 26   But when the Holy Spirit controls our lives he will produce this kind of fruit in us: love, joy, peace, patience, kindness, goodness, faithfulness, gentleness and self-control. . . .

If we are living now by the Holy Spirit's power, let us follow the Holy Spirit's leading in every part of our lives. Then we won't need to look for honours and popularity, which lead to jealousy and hard feelings.

James 4:5, 6, 7   Or what do you think the Scripture means when it says that the Holy Spirit, whom God has placed within us, watches over us with tender jealousy? But he gives us more and more strength to stand against all such evil longings. As the Scripture says, God gives strength to the humble, but sets himself against the proud and haughty.

So give yourselves humbly to God. Resist the devil and he will flee from you.

Romans 8:6, 9, 14, 16   Following after the Holy Spirit leads to life and peace, but following after the old nature leads to death.

But you are not like that. You are controlled by your new nature if you have the Spirit of God living in you. (And remember that if anyone doesn't have the Spirit of Christ living in him, he is not a Christian at all.)

For all who are led by the Spirit of God are sons of God.

For his Holy Spirit speaks to us deep in our hearts, and tells us that we really are God's children.

HONESTY

Deuteronomy 25:13–16   In all your transactions you must use accurate scales and honest measurements, so that you will have a long, good life in the land the Lord your God is giving you.

All who cheat with unjust weights and measurements are detestable to the Lord your God.

Psalm 51:6 You deserve honesty from the heart; yes, utter sincerity and truthfulness. Oh, give me this wisdom.

Proverbs 12:13 Lies will get any man into trouble, but honesty is its own defence.

Proverbs 16:8 A little, gained honestly, is better than great wealth gained by dishonest means.

Luke 16:10, 11 Unless you are honest in small matters, you won't be in large ones. If you cheat even a little, you won't be honest with greater responsibilities. And if you are untrustworthy about worldly wealth, who will trust you with the true riches of heaven?

Luke 19:8 Meanwhile, Zacchaeus stood before the Lord and said, "Sir, from now on I will give half my wealth to the poor, and if I find I have overcharged anyone on his taxes, I will give him back four times as much!"

Matthew 7:4, 5 Should you say, "Friend, let me help you get that speck out of your eye," when you can't even see because of the plank in your own? Hypocrite! First get rid of the plank. Then you can see to help your brother.

Romans 12:17 Never pay back evil for evil. Do things in such a way that everyone can see you are honest through and through.

JESUS CHRIST

Hebrews 2:10 And it was right and proper that God, who made everything for his own glory, should allow Jesus to suffer, for in doing this he was bringing vast multitudes of God's people to heaven; for his suffering made Jesus a perfect leader, one fit to bring them into their salvation.

Colossians 1:15–20 Christ is the exact likeness of the unseen God. He existed before God made anything at all, and, in fact, Christ himself is the Creator who made everything in heaven and earth, the things we can see and the things we can't; the spirit world with its kings and kingdoms, its rulers and authorities; all were made by Christ for his own use and glory. He was before all else began and it is his power that holds everything together. He is the head of the body made up of his people—that is, his church—which he began; and he is the leader of all who arise from the dead, so that he is first in everything; for God wanted all of himself to be in his Son.

It was through what his Son did that God cleared a path for everything to come to him—all things in heaven and on earth —for Christ's death on the cross has made peace with God for all by his blood.

Hebrews 5:8 Even though Jesus was God's Son, he had to learn from experience what it was like to obey, when obeying meant suffering.

Hebrews 13:8 Jesus Christ is the same yesterday, today, and forever.

1 John 2:23 For a person who doesn't believe in Christ, God's Son, can't have God the Father either. But he who has Christ, God's Son, has God the Father also.

John 15:4 Take care to live in me, and let me live in you. For a branch can't produce fruit when severed from the vine. Nor can you be fruitful apart from me.

Philippians 2:5–11 Your attitude should be the kind that was shown us by Jesus Christ, who, though he was God, did not demand and cling to his rights as God, but laid aside his mighty power and glory, taking the disguise of a slave and becoming like men. And he humbled himself even further, going so far as actually to die a criminal's death on the cross.

Yet it was because of this that God raised him up to the heights of heaven and gave him a name which is above every other name, that at the name of Jesus every knee shall bow in heaven and on earth and under the earth, and every tongue shall confess that Jesus Christ is Lord, to the glory of God the Father.

John 1:1–5   Before anything else existed, there was Christ, with God. He has always been alive and is himself God. He created everything there is—nothing exists that he didn't make. Eternal life is in him, and this life gives light to all mankind. His life is the light that shines through the darkness—and the darkness can never extinguish it.

John 10:30   I and the Father are one.

John 5:23   . . . So that everyone will honour the Son, just as they honour the Father. But if you refuse to honour God's Son, whom he sent to you, then you are certainly not honouring the Father.

John 6:38   For I have come here from heaven to do the will of God who sent me, not to have my own way.

JOY

Job 20:4, 5   Don't you realize that ever since man was first placed upon the earth, the triumph of the wicked has been short-lived, and the joy of the godless but for a moment?

Psalm 30:56   Weeping may go on all night, but in the morning there is joy.

2 Corinthians 4:18   . . . we do not look at what we can see at this moment, the troubles all around us, but we look forward to the joys in heaven which we have not yet seen. The troubles will soon be over, but the joys to come will last for ever.

Nehemiah 8:10 . . . the joy of the Lord is your strength.

Psalm 16:5, 9 The Lord himself is my inheritance, my prize. He is my food and drink, my highest joy! Heart, body and soul are filled with joy.

Psalm 69:32b All who seek for God shall live in joy.

Luke 2:10 . . . the angel reassured them. "Don't be afraid!" he said. "I bring you the most joyful news ever announced, and it is for everyone! The Saviour—yes, the Messiah, the Lord— has been born tonight in Bethlehem.

John 15:9–11 I have loved you even as the Father has loved me. Live within my love. When you obey me you are living in my love, just as I obey my Father and live in his love. I have told you this so that you will be filled with my joy. Yes, your cup of joy will overflow!

John 16:24b Ask, using my name, and you will receive, and your cup of joy will overflow.

Romans 4:8 Yes, what joy there is for anyone whose sins are no longer counted against him by the Lord.

Romans 14:17 . . . the important thing for us as Christians is . . . stirring up goodness and peace and joy from the Holy Spirit.

1 Thessalonians 5:16–18 Always be joyful. Always keep on praying. Always be thankful no matter what happens, for that is God's will for you who belong to Christ Jesus.

JUDGMENT

Job 2:22   Who can rebuke God, the supreme Judge?

Psalms 96:13   The Lord is coming to judge the earth; he will judge the nations fairly and with truth!

Ecclesiastes 12:14   For God will judge us for everything we do, including every hidden thing, good or bad.

Matthew 12:36   And I tell you this, that you must give account on Judgment Day for every idle word you speak.

John 12:48   All who reject me and my message will be judged at the Day of Judgment by the truths I have spoken.

Romans 2:12–16   He will punish sin wherever it is found. He will punish the heathen when they sin, even though they never had God's written laws, for down in their hearts they know right from wrong. God's laws are written within them; their own conscience accuses them, or sometimes excuses them. And God will punish the Jews for sinning because they have his written laws, but don't obey them. They know what is right but don't do it . . . The day will surely come when at God's command Jesus Christ will judge the secret life of everyone, their inmost thoughts and motives.

Romans 3:25   For God sent Christ Jesus to take the punishment for our sins and to end all God's anger against us.

Romans 5:18   Yes, Adam's sin brought punishment to all, but Christ's righteousness makes men right with God.

2 Corinthians 5:10   We must all stand before Christ to be judged and have our lives laid bare before him. Each of us will receive whatever he deserves for the good or bad things he has done in his earthly body.

Hebrews 9:27   . . . it is destined that men die only once, and after that comes the judgment . . .

1 Peter 1:17 ... remember that your heavenly Father to whom you pray has no favourites when he judges. He will judge you with perfect justice for everything you do; so act in reverent fear of him from now on until you get to heaven.

THE LAW

Galatians 3:19a Why were the laws given? They were added after the promise was given, to show men how guilty they are of breaking God's laws. But this system of law was to last only until the coming of Christ, the Child to whom God's promise was made.

Galatians 3:21b, 22 If we could be saved by his laws, then God would not have had to give us a different way to get out of the grip of sin—for the Scriptures insist we are all its prisoners. The only way out is through faith in Jesus Christ; the way of escape is open to all who believe him.

Ephesians 2:15b ... for he died to annul that whole system of Jewish laws.

LIFE IN CHRIST

1 Corinthians 1:30a For it is from God alone that you have your life through Christ Jesus.

1 Corinthians 2:15 The spiritual man has insight into everything, and that bothers and baffles the man of the world, who can't understand him at all.

Ephesians 1:3, 4 How we praise God, the Father of our Lord Jesus Christ, who has blessed us with every blessing in heaven because we belong to Christ.

Long ago, even before he made the world, God chose us to be his very own, through what Christ would do for us; he decided then to make us holy in his eyes, without a single fault —we who stand before him covered with his love.

Ephesians 3:17, 18, 19   And I pray that Christ will be more and more at home in your hearts, living within you as you trust in him. May your roots go down deep into the soil of God's marvellous love; and may you be able to feel and understand, as all God's children should, how long, how wide, how deep, and how high his love really is; and to experience this love for yourselves, though it is so great that you will never see the end of it or fully know or understand it. And so at last you will be filled up with God himself.

Philippians 3:8, 9   Yes, everything else is worthless when compared with the priceless gain of knowing Christ Jesus my Lord. I have put aside all else, counting it worth less than nothing, in order that I can have Christ, and become one with him, no longer counting on being saved by being good enough or by obeying God's laws, but by trusting Christ to save me; for God's way of making us right with himself depends on faith —counting on Christ alone.

Colossians 2:6   And now just as you trusted Christ to save you, trust him, too, for each day's problems; live in vital union with him.

2 Peter 1:2, 3   Do you want more and more of God's kindness and peace? Then learn to know him better and better. For as you know him better, he will give you, through his great power, everything you need for living a truly good life; he even shares his own glory and his own goodness with us!

1 John 1:6, 7   So if we say we are his friends, but go on living in spiritual darkness and sin, we are lying. But if we are living in the light of God's presence, just as Christ does, then we have wonderful fellowship and joy with each other, and the blood of Jesus his Son cleanses us from every sin.

Proverbs 22:17, 18, 19   Listen to this wise advice; follow it closely, for it will do you good, and you can pass it on to others: *Trust in the Lord.*

Matthew 5:13–16   You are the world's seasoning, to make it tolerable. If you lose your flavour, what will happen to the world? And you yourselves will be thrown out and trampled underfoot as worthless. You are the world's light—a city on a hill, glowing in the night for all to see. Don't hide your light! Let it shine for all; let your good deeds glow for all to see, so that they will praise your heavenly Father.

Matthew 10:38, 39   If you refuse to take up your cross and follow me, you are not worthy of being mine.

If you cling to your life, you will lose it; but if you give it up for me, you will save it.

Matthew 16:24, 25, 26   Then Jesus said to his disciples, "If anyone wants to be a follower of mine, let him deny himself and take up his cross and follow me. For anyone who keeps his life for himself shall lose it; and anyone who loses his life for me shall find it again. What profit is there if you gain the whole world—and lose eternal life? What can be compared with the value of eternal life?"

2 Corinthians 3:18   We Christians have no veil over our faces; we can be mirrors that brightly reflect the glory of the Lord. And as the Spirit of the Lord works within us, we become more and more like him.

LONELINESS

Genesis 2:18a   And the Lord God said, "It isn't good for man to be alone."

Ecclesiastes 4:9, 10   Two can accomplish more than twice as much as one, for the results can be much better. If one falls, the other pulls him up; but if a man falls when he is alone, he's in trouble.

Psalm 38:11, 21, 22 My loved ones and friends stay away . . . Even my own family stands at a distance. Don't leave me, Lord; don't go away! Come quickly! Help me, O my Saviour.

Psalm 40:1 I waited patiently for God to help me; then he listened and heard my cry.

John 14:15, 16, 18 "If you love me, obey me; and I will ask the Father and he will give you another Comforter, and he will never leave you . . . No, I will not abandon you or leave you as orphans—I will come to you."

John 16:32 "But the time is coming—in fact it is here—when you will be scattered, each one returning to his own home, leaving me alone. Yet I will not be alone, for the Father is with me."

Matthew 28:20b ". . . be sure of this—that I am with you always, even to the end of the world."

Words to the church:

1 Peter 3:8 And now this word to all of you: You should be like one big happy family, full of sympathy towards each other, loving one another with tender hearts and humble minds.

Hebrews 12:15a Look after each other so that not one of you will fail to find God's best blessings.

LOVE

Luke 14:26, 27, 33 "Anyone who wants to be my follower must love me far more than he does his own father, mother, wife, children, brothers, or sisters—yes, more than his own life—otherwise he cannot be my disciple. And no one can be my disciple who does not carry his own cross and follow me. So no one can become my disciple unless he first sits down and counts his blessings—and then renounces them all for me!"

1 John 4:8b, 9, 10, 16–19 God is love. God showed how much he loved us by sending his only Son into this wicked world to bring us eternal life through his death. In this act we see what real love is: It is not our love for God, but his love for us when he sent his Son to satisfy God's anger against our sins.

We know how much God loves us because we have felt his love and because we believe him when he tells us that he loves us dearly. God is love, and anyone who lives in love is living with God and God is living in him. And as we live with Christ, our love grows more perfect and complete; so we will not be ashamed and embarrassed at the day of judgment, but can face him with confidence and joy, because he loves us and we love him too.

We need have no fear of someone who loves us perfectly; his perfect love for us eliminates all dread of what he might do to us. If we are afraid, it is for fear of what he might do to us, and shows that we are not fully convinced that he really loves us. So you see, our love for him comes as a result of his loving us first.

1 Corinthians 13:4–8a Love is very patient and kind, never jealous or envious, never boastful or proud, never haughty or selfish or rude. Love does not demand its own way. It is not irritable or touchy. It does not hold grudges and will hardly even notice when others do it wrong. It is never glad about injustice, but rejoices whenever truth wins its way.

If you love someone you will be loyal to him no matter what the cost. You will always believe in him, always expect the best of him, and always stand your ground in defending him.

All the special gifts and powers from God will some day come to an end, but love goes on for ever.

THE MIND

1 Corinthians 2:11, 12   No one can really know what anyone else is thinking, or what he is really like, except that person himself. And no one can know God's thoughts except God's own Spirit. And God has actually given us his Spirit (not the world's spirit) to tell us about the wonderful free gifts of grace and blessing that God has given us.

1 Corinthians 2:16b   . . . We Christians actually do have within us something of the very thoughts and mind of Christ.

1 Corinthians 3:20   And again, in the book of Psalms, we are told that the Lord knows full well how the human mind reasons, and how foolish and futile it is.

Philippians 4:8b   Fix your thoughts on what is true and good and right. Think about things that are pure and lovely, and dwell on the fine, good things in others. Think about all you can praise God for and be glad about.

Romans 12:2   Don't copy the behaviour and customs of this world, but be a new and different person with a freshness in all you do and think. Then you will learn from your own experience how his ways will really satisfy you.

Proverbs 12:5   A good man's mind is filled with honest thoughts; an evil man's mind is crammed with lies.

Proverbs 16:23   From a wise mind comes careful and persuasive speech.

Psalm 119:165   Those who love your laws have great peace of heart and mind and do not stumble.

Psalm 94:19   Lord, when doubts fill my mind, when my heart is in turmoil, quiet me and give me renewed hope and cheer.

Psalm 51:10   Create in me a new, clean heart, O God, filled with clean thoughts and right desires.

MIRACLES

Psalm 40:5   O Lord my God, many and many a time you have done great miracles for us, and we are ever in your thoughts. Who else can do such glorious things? No one else can be compared with you. There isn't time to tell of all your wonderful deeds.

Psalm 66:5   Come, see the glorious things God has done. What marvellous miracles happen to his people!

Mark 16:17, 18   "And those who believe shall use my authority to cast out demons, and they shall speak new languages. They will even be able to handle snakes with safety, and if they drink anything poisonous, it will not hurt them, and they will be able to place their hands on the sick and heal them."

NATURAL MAN

1 Corinthians 1:20, 21   So what about these wise men, these scholars, these brilliant debaters of this world's great affairs? God has made them all look foolish, and shown their wisdom to be useless nonsense. For God in his wisdom saw to it that the world would never find God through human brilliance, and then he stepped in and saved all those who believed his message, which the world calls foolish and silly.

1 Corinthians 1:27   God has deliberately chosen to use ideas the world considers foolish and of little worth in order to shame those people considered by the world as wise and great.

1 Corinthians 2:14   But the man who hasn't the Spirit can't understand and can't accept these thoughts from God, which the Holy Spirit teaches us. They sound foolish to him, because only those who have the Holy Spirit within them can understand what the Holy Spirit means. Others just can't take it in.

1 Corinthians 3:19   For the wisdom of this world is foolishness to God. As it says in the book of Job, God uses man's own brilliance to trap him; he stumbles over his own "wisdom" and falls.

Ephesians 4:18, 19   Live no longer as the unsaved do, for they are blinded and confused. Their closed hearts are full of darkness; they are far away from the life of God because they have shut their minds against him, and they cannot understand his ways. They don't care any more about right and wrong and have given themselves over to impure ways. They stop at nothing, being driven by their evil minds and reckless lusts.

Psalm 36:1, 2   Sin lurks deep in the hearts of the wicked, forever urging them on to evil deeds. They have no fear of God to hold them back. Instead, in their conceit, they think they can hide their evil deeds and not get caught.

John 3:18, 19, 20   There is no eternal doom awaiting those who trust him to save them. But those who don't trust him have already been tried and condemned for not believing in the only son of God. Their sentence is based on this fact: that the Light from heaven came into the world, but they loved the darkness more than the Light, for their deeds were evil. They hated the heavenly Light because they wanted to sin in the darkness. They stayed away from that Light for fear their sins would be exposed and they would be punished.

NEEDS SUPPLIED

2 Corinthians 9:8 God is able to make it up to you by giving you everything you need and more, so that there will not only be enough for your own needs, but plenty left over to give joyfully to others.

Philippians 4:11, 12, 13 Not that I was ever in need, for I have learned how to get along happily whether I have much or little. I know how to live on almost nothing or with everything. I have learned the secret of contentment in every situation, whether it be a full stomach or hunger, plenty or want; for I can do everything God asks me to with the help of Christ who gives me the strength and power.

Matthew 6:25, 26, 31–34 So my counsel is: Don't worry about *things*—food, drink, money and clothes. For you already have life and a body—and they are far more important than what to eat and wear. Look at the birds! They don't worry about what to eat—they don't need to sow or reap or store up food —for your heavenly Father feeds them. And you are far more valuable to him than they are.

So don't worry at all about having enough food and clothing. Why be like the heathen? For they take pride in all these things and are deeply concerned about them. But your heavenly Father already knows perfectly well that you need them, and he will give them to you if you give him first place in your life.

So don't be anxious about tomorrow. God will take care of your tomorrow too. Live one day at a time.

Matthew 7:7, 8, 11 Ask, and you will be given what you ask for. Seek, and you will find. Knock, and the door will be opened. For everyone who asks, receives. Anyone who seeks, finds. If only you will knock, the door will open. And if you hardhearted, sinful men know how to give good gifts to your children, won't your Father in heaven even more certainly give good gifts to those who ask him for them?

NEW CHRISTIANS

1 Corinthians 3:1a, 3a I have been talking to you as though you were still just babies in the Christian life, who are not following the Lord, but your own desires. For you are still only baby Christians, controlled by your own desires, not God's.

1 Corinthians 5:8 So let us feast upon him and grow strong in the Christian life, leaving entirely behind us the cancerous old life with all its hatreds and wickedness. Let us feast instead upon the pure bread of honour and sincerity and truth.

1 Corinthians 7:20, 24 Usually a person should keep on with the work he was doing when God called him. Whatever situation a person is in when he becomes a Christian, let him stay there, for now the Lord is there to help him.

Ephesians 4:17–20 Let me say this, then, speaking for the Lord: live no longer as the unsaved do, for they are blinded and confused. Their closed hearts are full of darkness; they are far away from the life of God because they have shut their minds against him, and they cannot understand his ways. They don't care any more about right and wrong and have given themselves over to impure ways. They stop at nothing, being driven by their evil minds and reckless lusts. But that isn't the way Christ taught you!

Ephesians 2:19 Now you are no longer strangers to God and foreigners to heaven, but you are members of God's very own family, citizens of God's country, and you belong in God's household with every other Christian.

Colossians 3:10, 11, 12 You are living a brand new kind of life that is continually learning more and more of what is right, and trying constantly to be more and more like Christ who created this new life within you. In this new life one's nationality or race or education or social position is unimportant;

such things mean nothing. Whether a person has Christ is what matters and he is equally available to all.

Since you have been chosen by God who has given you this new kind of life, and because of his deep love and concern for you, you should practise tenderhearted mercy and kindness to others. Don't worry about making a good impression on them but be ready to suffer quietly and patiently.

1 Peter 4:3, 4 You have had enough in the past of the evil things the godless enjoy—sexual sin, lust, getting drunk, wild parties, drinking bouts, and the worship of idols—which leads to other terrible sins.

Of course, your former friends will be very surprised when you don't eagerly join them any more in the wicked things they do, and they will laugh at you in contempt and scorn.

Romans 6:22 But now you are free from the power of sin and are slaves of God, and his benefits to you include holiness and everlasting life.

NEW LIFE

2 Corinthians 5:17 When someone becomes a Christian he becomes a brand new person inside. He is not the same any more. A new life has begun!

Galatians 2:20 I have been crucified with Christ: and I myself no longer live, but Christ lives in me. And the real life I now have within this body is a result of my trusting in the Son of God, who loved me and gave himself for me.

1 Peter 1:23 For you have a new life. It was not passed on to you from your parents, for the life they gave you will fade away. This new one will last forever, for it comes from Christ, God's ever-living message to men.

Colossians 3:10, 11   You are living a brand new kind of life that is continually learning more and more of what is right, and trying constantly to be more and more like Christ who created this new life within you. In this new life one's nationality or race or education or social position is unimportant; such things mean nothing. Whether a person has Christ is what matters, and he is equally available to all.

Matthew 16:24, 25, 26   Then Jesus said to the disciples, "If anyone wants to be a follower of mine, let him deny himself and take up his cross and follow me. For anyone who keeps his life for himself shall lose it; and anyone who loses his life for me shall find it again. What profit is there if you gain the whole world—and lose eternal life? What can be compared with the value of eternal life?"

Romans 3:21, 22, 23   But now God has shown us a different way to heaven—not by "being good enough" and trying to keep his laws, but by a new way (though not new, really, for the Scriptures told about it long ago). Now God says he will accept and acquit us—declare us "not guilty"—if we trust Jesus Christ to take away our sins. And we all can be saved in this same way, by coming to Christ, no matter who we are or what we have been like. Yes, all have sinned; all fall short of God's glorious ideal.

THE OCCULT

Leviticus 20:6   I will set my face against anyone who consults mediums and wizards instead of me, and I will cut that person off from his people.

Deuteronomy 18:10b, 11   No Israeli may practise black magic, or call on the evil spirits for aid, or be a fortune teller, or be a serpent charmer, medium, or wizard, or call up the spirits of the dead. Anyone doing these things is an object of horror and disgust to the Lord, and it is because the nations do these things that the Lord your God will displace them.

2 Kings 21:6b   He (Manasseh) practised black magic and used fortune-telling, and patronized mediums and wizards. So the Lord was very angry . . .

1 Chronicles 10:13   Saul died for his disobedience to the Lord and because he had consulted a medium, and did not ask the Lord for guidance.

Matthew 10:1   Jesus called his twelve disciples to him, and gave them authority to cast out evil spirits . . .

Acts 19:18, 19   Many of the believers who had been practising black magic confessed their deeds and brought their incantation books and charms and burned them at a public bonfire.

Galatians 5:19, 20   But when you follow your own wrong inclinations your lives will produce these evil results . . . idolatry, spiritism (that is, encouraging the activity of demons) . . .

OLD EVIL NATURE

Galatians 5:16, 17   I advise you to obey only the Holy Spirit's instructions. He will tell you where to go and what to do, and then you won't always be doing the wrong things your evil nature wants you to. For we naturally love to do evil things that are just the opposite of the things that the Holy Spirit tells us to do; and the good things we want to do when the Spirit has his way with us are just the opposite of our natural desires. These two forces within us are constantly fighting each other to win control over us, and our wishes are never free from their pressures.

Galatians 5:24   Those who belong to Christ have nailed their natural evil desires to his cross and crucified them there.

Galatians 5:19, 20, 21   But when you follow your own wrong inclinations your lives will produce these evil results: impure thoughts, eagerness for lustful pleasure, idolatry, spiritism (that is, encouraging the activity of demons), hatred and fighting, jealousy and anger, constant effort to get the best for yourself, complaints and criticisms, the feeling that everyone else is wrong except those in your own little group—and there will be wrong doctrine, envy, murder, drunkenness, wild parties, and all that sort of thing. Let me tell you again as I have before, that anyone living that sort of life will not inherit the kingdom of God.

PATIENCE

Psalm 37:7, 9b   Rest in the Lord; wait patiently for him to act. . . . those who trust in the Lord shall be given every blessing.

Psalm 40:1   I waited patiently for God to help me; then he listened and heard my cry.

Romans 2:7a   He will give eternal life to those who patiently do the will of God.

Romans 5:3, 4   We can rejoice, too, when we run into problems and trials, for we know that they are good for us —they help us learn to be patient. And patience develops strength of character in us and helps us trust God more each time we use it until finally our hope and faith are strong and steady.

Romans 15:5   May God who gives patience, steadiness, and encouragement help you to live in complete harmony with each other—each with the attitude of Christ towards the other.

Ephesians 4:2   Be humble and gentle. Be patient with each other, making allowance for each other's faults because of your love.

Hebrews 10:36   You need to keep on patiently doing God's will if you want him to do for you all that he has promised.

Hebrews 12:1b   . . . let us run with patience the particular race that God has set before us.

James 1:3, 4   When the way is rough, your patience has a chance to grow. So let it grow and don't try to squirm out of your problems. For when your patience is finally in full bloom then you will be ready for anything, strong in character, full and complete.

2 Peter 1:6   Learn to put aside your own desires so that you will become patient and godly, gladly letting God have his way with you.

PEACE

Philippians 4:6, 7   Don't worry about anything; instead, pray about everything; tell God your needs and don't forget to thank him for his answers. If you do this you will experience God's peace, which is far more wonderful than the human mind can understand. His peace will keep your thoughts and your hearts quiet and at rest as you trust in Christ Jesus.

John 14:27   I am leaving you with a gift—peace of mind and heart! And the peace I give isn't fragile like the peace the world gives. So don't be troubled or afraid.

John 16:33   I have told you all this so that you will have peace of heart and mind. Here on earth you will have many trials and sorrows; but take courage, I have overcome the world.

POWER

2 Corinthians 12:9, 10   "I am with you; that is all you need. My power shows up best in weak people." Now I am glad to boast about how weak I am; I am glad to be a living demonstration of Christ's power, instead of showing off my own power and abilities. Since I know it is all for Christ's good, I am quite happy about "the thorn", and about insults and hardships, persecutions and difficulties; for when I am weak, then I am strong—the less I have, the more I depend on him.

Philippians 4:13   For I can do everything God asks me to with the help of Christ who gives me the strength and power.

Isaiah 40:29   He gives power to the tired and worn out, and strength to the weak.

Psalm 147:5   How great he is! His power is absolute! His understanding is unlimited.

PRAISE

Psalm 16:11   You have let me experience the joys of life and the exquisite pleasures of your own eternal presence.

Psalm 18:1   Lord, how I love you! For you have done such tremendous things for me.

Psalm 32   What happiness for those whose guilt has been forgiven! What joys when sins are covered over! What relief for those who have confessed their sins and God has cleared their record.

There was a time when I wouldn't admit what a sinner I was. But my dishonesty made me miserable and filled my days with frustration. All day and all night your hand was heavy on me. My strength evaporated like water on a sunny day until I finally admitted all my sins to you and stopped trying to hide them. I said to myself, "I will confess them to the Lord." And you forgave me! All my guilt is gone.

Now I say that each believer should confess his sins to God when he is aware of them, while there is time to be forgiven. Judgment will not touch him if he does.

You are my hiding place from every storm of life; you even keep me from getting into trouble! You surround me with songs of victory. I will instruct you (says the Lord) and guide you along the best pathway for your life; I will advise you and watch your progress. Don't be like a senseless horse or mule that has to have a bit in its mouth to keep it in line! Many sorrows come to the wicked, but abiding love surrounds those who trust in the Lord. So rejoice in him, all those who are his, and shout for joy, all those who try to obey him.

Psalm 86   Bend down and hear my prayer, O Lord, and answer me, for I am deep in trouble.

Protect me from death, for I try to follow all your laws. Save me, for I am serving you and trusting you. Be merciful, O Lord, for I am looking up to you in constant hope. Give me happiness, O Lord, for I worship only you. O Lord, you are so good and kind, so ready to forgive; so full of mercy for all who ask your aid. Listen closely to my prayer, O God. Hear my urgent cry. I will call to you whenever trouble strikes, and you will help me.

Where among the heathen gods is there a god like you? Where are their miracles? All the nations—and you made each one—will come and bow before you, Lord, and praise your great and holy name. For you are great, and do great miracles. You alone are God.

Tell me where you want me to go and I will go there. May every fibre of my being unite in reverence to your name. With all my heart I will praise you. I will give glory to your name forever, for you love me so much! You are constantly so kind! You have rescued me from deepest hell.

O God, proud and insolent men defy me; violent, godless men are trying to kill me. But you are merciful and gentle, Lord, slow in getting angry, full of constant lovingkindness and of truth; so look down in pity and grant strength to your servant and save me. Send me a sign of your favour. When those who hate me see it they will lose face because you help and comfort me.

Psalm 103:1–7   I bless the holy name of God with all my heart. Yes, I will bless the Lord and not forget the glorious things he does for me.

He forgives all my sins. He heals me. He ransoms me from hell. He surrounds me with lovingkindness and tender mercies. He fills my life with good things! My youth is renewed like the eagle's! He gives justice to all who are treated unfairly. He revealed his will and nature to Moses and the people of Israel.

Psalm 139:1–18   O Lord, you have examined my heart and know everything about me. You know when I sit or stand. When far away you know my every thought. You chart the path ahead of me, and tell me where to stop and rest. Every moment, you know where I am. You know what I am going to say before I even say it. You both precede and follow me, and place your hand of blessing on my head.

This is too glorious, too wonderful to believe! I can *never* be lost to your Spirit! I can *never* get away from my God! If I go up to heaven, you are there; if I go down to the place of the dead, you are there. If I ride the morning winds to the farthest oceans, even there your hand will guide me, your strength will support me. If I try to hide in the darkness, the night becomes light around me. For even darkness cannot hide from God; to you the night shines as bright as day. Darkness and light are both alike to you.

You made all the delicate, inner parts of my body, and knit them together in my mother's womb. Thank you for making me so wonderfully complex! It is amazing to think about. Your workmanship is marvellous—and how well I know it. You were there while I was being formed in utter seclusion! You saw me before I was born and scheduled each day of my life before I began to breathe. Every day was recorded in your Book!

How precious it is, Lord, to realize that you are thinking about me constantly! I can't even count how many times a day your thoughts turn towards me! And when I wake in the morning, you are still thinking of me!

Psalm 9:1 O Lord, I will praise you with all my heart, and tell everyone about the marvellous things you do.

Psalm 18:1 Lord, how I love you! For you have done such tremendous things for me.

Psalm 35:10a From the bottom of my heart praise rises to him. Where is his equal in all of heaven and earth?

Psalm 63:3, 4 Your love and kindness are better to me than life itself. How I praise you! I will bless you as long as I live, lifting up my hands to you in prayer.

Psalm 71:8, 16 All day long I'll praise and honour you, O God, for all that you have done for me.

I walk in the strength of the Lord God. I tell everyone that you alone are just and good.

Psalm 103:2, 5, 8, 9, 12, 13 Yes, I will bless the Lord and not forget the glorious things he does for me.

He fills my life with good things! My youth is renewed like the eagle's!

He is merciful and tender towards those who don't deserve it; he is slow to get angry and full of kindness and love. He never bears a grudge, nor remains angry forever.

He has removed our sins as far away from us as the east is from the west. He is like a father to us, tender and sympathetic to those who reverence him.

Psalm 106:2   Who can ever list the glorious miracles of God? Who can ever praise him half enough?

1 Thessalonians 5:18   Always be thankful no matter what happens, for that is God's will for you who belong to Christ Jesus.

PRAYER

James 5:16   Admit your faults to one another and pray for each other so that you may be healed. The earnest prayer of a righteous man has great power and wonderful results.

Romans 8:26, 27   . . . the Holy Spirit helps us with our daily problems and in our praying. For we don't even know what we should pray for, nor how to pray as we should; but the Holy Spirit prays for us with such feeling that it cannot be expressed in words. And the Father who knows all hearts knows, of course, what the Spirit is saying as he pleads for us in harmony with God's own will.

1 John 5:14, 15   And we are sure of this, that he will listen to us whenever we ask him for anything in line with his will. And if we really know he is listening when we talk to him and make our requests, then we can be sure that he will answer us.

John 15:7   But if you stay in me and obey my commands, you may ask any request you like, and it will be granted!

Psalm 130:3, 4   Lord, if you keep in mind our sins then who can ever get an answer to his prayers? But you forgive! What an awesome thing this is!

Matthew 6:7, 8   Don't recite the same prayer over and over as the heathen do, who think prayers are answered if they are repeated again and again. Remember, your Father knows exactly what you need even before you ask him!

Matthew 18:19, 20 "I also tell you this—if two of you agree down here on earth concerning anything you ask for, my Father in heaven will do it for you. For where two or three gather together because they are mine, I will be there among them."

PROBLEMS, TROUBLES, DIFFICULTIES

Romans 8:38, 39 For I am convinced that nothing can ever separate us from his love. Death can't, and life can't. The angels won't, and all the powers of hell itself cannot keep God's love away. Our fears for today, our worries about tomorrow, or where we are—high above the sky, or in the deepest ocean —nothing will ever be able to separate us from the love of God demonstrated by our Lord Jesus Christ when he died for us.

James 1:2, 3, 4 Dear brothers, is your life full of difficulties and temptations? Then be happy, for when the way is rough, your patience has a chance to grow. So let it grow, and don't try to squirm out of your problems. For when your patience is finally in full bloom, then you will be ready for anything, strong in character, full and complete.

1 Peter 4:12, 13 Dear friends, don't be bewildered or surprised when you go through the fiery trials ahead, for this is no strange, unusual thing that is going to happen to you. Instead, be really glad—because these trials will make you partners with Christ in his suffering, and afterwards you will have the wonderful joy of sharing his glory in that coming day when it will be displayed.

Romans 5:3, 4 We can rejoice, too, when we run into problems and trials for we know that they are good for us—they help us learn to be patient. And patience develops strength of character in us and helps us trust God more each time we use it until finally our hope and faith are strong and steady.

Psalm 57:1   O God, have pity, for I am trusting you! I will hide beneath the shadow of your wings until this storm is past.

Romans 8:28   And we know that all that happens to us is working for our good if we love God and are fitting into his plans.

Psalm 34:1, 17   I will praise the Lord no matter what happens. I will constantly speak of his glories and grace. Yes, the Lord hears the good man when he calls to him for help, and saves him out of all his troubles.

Psalms 37:34   Don't be impatient for the Lord to act! Keep travelling steadily along his pathway and in due season he will honour you with every blessing.

Psalm 71:20   You have let me sink down deep in desperate problems. But you will bring me back to life again, up from the depths of the earth.

Proverbs 24:10   You are a poor specimen if you can't stand the pressure of adversity.

Proverbs 27:12   A sensible man watches for problems ahead and prepares to meet them. The simpleton never looks, and suffers the consequences.

Psalm 77:1–9, 11–14   I cry to the Lord; I call and call to him. Oh, that he would listen. I am in deep trouble and I need his help so badly. All night long I pray, lifting my hands to heaven, pleading. There can be no joy for me until he acts. I think of God and moan, overwhelmed with longing for his help. I cannot sleep until you act. I am too distressed even to pray!

I keep thinking of the good old days of the past, long since ended. Then my nights were filled with joyous songs. I search my soul and meditate upon the difference now. Has the Lord rejected me forever? Will he never again be favourable? Is his lovingkindness gone forever? Has his promise failed? Has he forgotten to be kind to one so undeserving? Has he slammed the door in anger on his love?

I recall the many miracles he did for me so long ago. Those wonderful deeds are constantly in my thoughts. I cannot stop thinking about them.

O God, your ways are holy. Where is there any other as mighty as you? You are the God of miracles and wonders! You still demonstrate your awesome power.

RACE

1 Samuel 16:7   The Lord said to Samuel, "Don't judge by a man's face or height. . . . I don't make decisions the way you do! Men judge by outward appearance, but I look at a man's thoughts and intentions."

Isaiah 60:1, 3   . . . Let your light shine for all the nations to see. All nations will come to your light . . .

Matthew 28:19   Therefore go and make disciples in all the nations . . .

Acts 10:28   . . . God has shown me in a vision that I should never think of anyone as inferior.

Romans 2:9–11   There will be sorrow and suffering for Jews and Gentiles alike who keep on sinning, but there will be glory and honour and peace from God for all who obey him, whether they are Jews or Gentiles. For God treats everyone the same.

Galatians 3:28   We are no longer Jews or Greeks or slaves or free men or even merely men or women, but we are all the same—we are Christians; we are one in Christ Jesus.

Colossians 3:11 In this new life one's nationality or race or education or social position is unimportant; such things mean nothing. Whether a person has Christ is what matters, and he is equally available to all.

Revelation 5:9 . . . you were slain, (Jesus) and your blood has bought people from every nation as gifts for God.

RELATIONSHIPS WITH PEOPLE

1 Corinthians 9:21, 22 When with the heathen I agree with them as much as I can, except of course that I must always do what is right as a Christian. And so, by agreeing, I can win their confidence and help them too.

When I am with those whose consciences bother them easily, I don't act as though I know it all and don't say they are foolish; the result is that they are willing to let me help them. Yes, whatever a person is like, I try to find common ground with him so that he will let me tell him about Christ and let Christ save him.

Galatians 6:1, 2, 3 Dear brothers, if a Christian is overcome by some sin, you who are godly should gently and humbly help him back on to the right path, remembering that next time it might be one of you who is in the wrong. Share each other's troubles and problems, and so obey our Lord's command. If anyone thinks he is too great to stoop to this, he is fooling himself. He is really a nobody.

Colossians 3:12–15. Since you have been chosen by God who has given you this new kind of life, and because of his deep love and concern for you, you should practise tenderhearted mercy and kindness to others. Don't worry about making a good impression on them but be ready to suffer quietly and patiently. Be gentle and ready to forgive; never hold grudges. Remember, the Lord forgave you, so you must forgive others.

Most of all, let love guide your life, for then the whole church will stay together in perfect harmony. Let the peace of heart which comes from Christ be always present in your hearts and lives, for this is your responsibility and privilege as members of his body. And always be thankful.

Titus 3:9a Don't get involved in arguing over unanswerable questions and controversial theological ideas.

Hebrews 13:3 Don't forget about those in jail. Suffer with them as though you were there yourself. Share the sorrow of those being ill-treated, for you know what they are going through.

James 5:19, 20 Dear brothers, if anyone has slipped away from God and no longer trusts the Lord, and someone helps him understand the Truth again, that person who brings him back to God will have saved a wandering soul from death, bringing about the forgiveness of his many sins.

2 Peter 1:6, 7, 8 Learn to put aside your own desires so that you will become patient and godly, gladly letting God have his way with you. This will make possible the next step, which is for you to enjoy other people and to like them, and finally you will grow to love them deeply. The more you go on in this way, the more you will grow strong spiritually and become fruitful and useful to our Lord Jesus Christ.

1 John 1:7a But if we are living in the light of God's presence, just as Christ does, then we have wonderful fellowship and joy with each other.

Galatians 6:10 Whenever we can we should always be kind to everyone, and especially to our Christian brothers.

Ephesians 4:2, 3 Be humble and gentle. Be patient with each other, making allowance for each other's faults because of your love. Try always to be led along together by the Holy Spirit, and so be at peace with one another.

RICHES

1 Chronicles 29:12   Riches and honour come from you above, and you are the Ruler of all mankind.

Psalm 49:6, 7   They trust in their wealth and boast about how rich they are, yet not one of them, though rich as kings, can ransom his own brother from the penalty of sin!

Psalm 62:10, 11   Don't become rich by extortion and robbery. And don't let the rich men be proud.

Proverbs 11:4   Your riches won't help you on Judgment Day; only righteousness counts then.

Matthew 6:24   You cannot serve two masters: God and money. For you will hate one and love the other, or else the other way round.

Mark 4:18, 19   The thorny ground represents the hearts of people who listen to the Good News and receive it, but all too quickly the attractions of this world, and the delights of wealth, and the search for success and the lure of attractive things come in and crowd out God's message from their hearts, so that no crop is produced.

Mark 10:24, 25   . . . Jesus said it again: "How hard it is for those who trust in riches to enter the Kingdom of God. It is easier for a camel to go through the eye of a needle than for a rich man to enter the Kingdom of God."

1 Timothy 6:17–19   Tell those who are rich not to be proud and not to trust in their money, which will soon be gone, but their pride and trust should be in the living God who always richly gives us all we need for our enjoyment. Tell them to use their money to do good. They should be rich in good works and should give happily to those in need, always being ready to share with others whatever God has given them. By doing this they will be storing up real treasure for themselves in heaven— it is the only safe investment for eternity! And they will be living a fruitful Christian life down here as well.

SATAN

Isiah 14:12–14   How you are fallen from heaven, O Lucifer, son of the morning! How you are cut down to the ground— mighty though you were against the nations of the world. For you said to yourself, "I will ascend to heaven and rule the angels. I will take the highest throne. I will preside on the Mount of Assembly far away in the north. I will climb to the highest heavens and be like the Most High."

1 Peter 5:8   Be careful—watch out for attacks from Satan, your great enemy. He prowls around like a hungry, roaring lion, looking for some victim to tear apart. Stand firm when he attacks. Trust the Lord. And remember that other Christians all around the world are going through these sufferings too.

Ephesians 6:10–17   Last of all I want to remind you that your strength must come from the Lord's mighty power within you. Put on all of God's armour so that you will be able to stand safe against the strategies and tricks of Satan. For we are not fighting against people made of flesh and blood, but against persons without bodies—the evil rulers of the unseen world, those mighty satanic beings and great evil princes of darkness who rule this world; and against huge numbers of wicked spirits in the spirit world.

So use every piece of God's armour to resist the enemy whenever he attacks, and when it is all over, you will still be standing up.

But to do this, you will need the strong belt of truth and the breastplate of God's approval. Wear shoes that are able to speed you on as you preach the Good News of peace with God. In every battle you will need faith as your shield to stop the fiery arrows aimed at you by Satan. And you will need the helmet of salvation and the sword of the Spirit—which is the Word of God.

2 Corinthians 11:14   Satan can change himself into an angel of light.

1 John 5:19   We know that we are children of God and that all the rest of the world around us is under Satan's power and control.

SECURITY

Psalm 61:2, 3   When my heart is faint and overwhelmed, lead me to the mighty towering Rock of safety. For you are my refuge, a high tower where my enemies can never reach me.

Psalm 46:1, 2   God is our refuge and strength, a tested help in times of trouble. And so we need not fear even if the world blows up, and the mountains crumble into the sea.

Deuteronomy 33:27   The eternal God is your Refuge, And underneath are the everlasting arms.

Isaiah 49:15, 16   . . . Can a mother forget her little child and not have love for her own son? Yet even if that should be, I will not forget you. See, I have tattooed your name upon my palm . . ."

Hebrews 13:5b   For God has said, "I will never, NEVER fail you nor forsake you."

John 10:27–29 My sheep recognize my voice, and I know them, and they follow me. I give them eternal life and they shall never perish. No one shall snatch them away from me, for my Father has given them to me, and he is more powerful than anyone else, so no one can kidnap them from me.

Matthew 10:29–31 Not one sparrow—what do they cost— two for a penny? —can fall to the ground without your Father knowing it. And the very hairs of your head are all numbered. So don't worry! You are more valuable to him than many sparrows.

Romans 8:38 For I am convinced that nothing can ever separate us from his love. Death can't, and life can't. The angels won't, and all the powers of hell itself cannot keep God's love away.

SELF-IMAGE

Genesis 1:26 Then God said, "Let us make a man—someone like ourselves, to be the master of all life upon the earth and in the skies and in the seas."

Ephesians 2:10a It is God himself who has made us what we are and given us new lives from Christ Jesus.

2 Corinthians 3:18 We Christians have no veil over our faces; we can be mirrors that brightly reflect the glory of the Lord. And as the Spirit of the Lord works within us, we become more and more like him.

2 Corinthians 5:21 For God took the sinless Christ and poured into him our sins. Then, in exchange, he poured God's goodness into us!

Galatians 2:19b I came to realize that acceptance with God comes by believing in Christ.

Galatians 5:25, 26 If we are living now by the Holy Spirit's power, let us follow the Holy Spirit's leading in every part of our lives. Then we won't need to look for honours and popularity, which lead to jealousy and hard feelings.

Galatians 6:4 Let everyone be sure that he is doing his very best, for then he will have the personal satisfaction of work well done, and won't need to compare himself with someone else.

SEX

Genesis 2:23, 24 "This is it," Adam exclaimed. "She is part of my own bone and flesh. Her name is 'woman' because she was taken out of a man." This explains why a man leaves his father and mother and is joined to his wife in such a way that the two become one person.

Matthew 19:4–6 It is written that at the beginning God created man and woman, and that a man should leave his father and mother, and be forever united to his wife. The two shall become one—no longer two, but one. No man may divorce what God has joined together.

1 Corinthians 11:11 But remember that in God's plan men and women need each other.

Proverbs 18:22 The man who finds a wife finds a good thing; she is a blessing to him from the Lord.

Colossians 3:18, 19 You wives, submit yourselves to your husbands, for that is what the Lord has planned for you. And you husbands must be loving and kind to your wives and not bitter against them, nor harsh.

Proverbs 5:18, 19 Let your manhood be a blessing; rejoice in the wife of your youth. Let her charms and tender embrace satisfy you. Let her love alone fill you with delight.

Proverbs 6:29, 32 . . . The man who commits adultery with another's wife . . . shall not go unpunished for this sin. [He] is an utter fool, for he destroys his own soul.

Proverbs 31:10 If you can find a truly good wife, she is worth more than precious gems!

Proverbs 4:23–26 Above all else, guard your affections. For they influence everything else in your life. Spurn the careless kiss of a prostitute. Stay far from her. Look straight ahead; don't even turn your head to look. Watch your step. Stick to the path and be safe.

Proverbs 7:24–27 Listen to me, young men, and not only listen but obey; don't let your desires get out of hand; don't let yourself think about [a prostitute]. Don't go near her; stay away from where she walks, in case she should tempt you and seduce you. For she has been the ruin of multitudes—a vast host of men have been her victims. If you want to find the road to hell, look for her house.

Song of Solomon 8:7 Many waters cannot quench the flame of love, neither can the floods drown it. If a man tried to buy it with everything he owned, he couldn't do it.

Philippians 4:8 Fix your thoughts on what is true and good and right. Think about things that are pure and lovely, and dwell on the fine, good things in others. Think about all you can praise God for and be glad about.

1 Corinthians 6:13b–20 Sexual sin is never right: our bodies were made not for that, but for the Lord, and the Lord wants to fill our bodies with himself. And God is going to raise our bodies from the dead by his power just as he raised up the Lord Jesus Christ. Don't you realize that your bodies are actually parts and members of Christ? So should I take part of Christ and join him to a prostitute? Never! And don't you know that if a man joins himself to a prostitute she becomes a part of him and he becomes a part of her? For God tells us in the Scripture that

in his sight the two become one person. But if you give yourself to the Lord, you and Christ are joined together as one
person.

That is why I say you should steer clear of sexual immorality.
No other sin affects the body as this one does. When you sin in
this way it is against your own body. Haven't you yet learned
that your body is the home of the Holy Spirit God gave you,
and that he lives within you? Your own body does not belong
to you. For God has bought you with a great price. So use every
part of your body to give glory back to God, because he owns
it.

1 Corinthians 10:13, 24 The wrong desires that come into
your life aren't anything new and different. Many others have
faced exactly the same problems before you. And no temptation
is irresistible. You can trust God to keep the temptation from
becoming so strong that you can't stand up against it, for he has
promised this and will do what he says. He will show you how
to escape temptation's power so that you can bear up patiently
against it.

Don't think only of yourself. Try to think of the other fellow
too, and what is best for him.

Psalm 119:73 You made my body, Lord; now give me sense to
heed your laws.

SHARING—GIVING

2 Corinthians 9:7, 8, 11a Every one must make up his own
mind as to how much he should give. Don't force anyone to
give more than he really wants to, for cheerful givers are the
ones God prizes. God is able to make it up to you by giving you
everything you need and more, so that there will not only be

81

enough for your own needs, but plenty left over to give joyfully to others.

Yes, God will give you much so that you can give away much.

Proverbs 11:24, 25 It is possible to give away and become richer! It is also possible to hold on too tightly and lose everything. Yes, the liberal man shall be rich! By watering others, he waters himself.

Proverbs 22:9 Happy is the generous man, the one who feeds the poor.

Matthew 5:42; 6:1, 3 Give to those who ask, and don't turn away from those who want to borrow.

Take care! Don't do your good deeds publicly, to be admired, for then you will lose the reward from your Father in heaven. But when you do a kindness to someone, do it secretly —don't tell your left hand what your right hand is doing.

Luke 6:30, 38 Give what you have to anyone who asks you for it; and when things are taken away from you, don't worry about getting them back.

For if you give, you will get. Your gift will return to you in full and overflowing measure, pressed down, shaken together to make room for more, and running over. Whatever measure you use to give—large or small—will be used to measure what is given back to you.

SIN

Romans 5:12 When Adam sinned, sin entered the entire human race. His sin spread death throughout all the world, so everything began to grow old and die, for all sinned.

James 4:9, 10 Let there be tears for the wrong things you have done. Let there be sorrow and sincere grief. Let there be sadness instead of laughter, and gloom instead of joy. Then when you feel your worthlessness before the Lord, he will lift you up, encourage and help you.

James 4:17 Remember, too, that knowing what is right to do and then not doing it is sin.

2 Peter 2:20, 21, 22 And when a person has escaped from the wicked ways of the world by learning about our Lord and Saviour Jesus Christ, and then gets tangled up with sin and becomes its slave again, he is worse off than he was before. It would be better if he had never known about Christ at all than to learn of him and then afterwards turn his back on the holy commandments that were given to him. There is an old saying that "A dog comes back to what he has vomited, and a pig is washed only to come back and wallow in the mud again." That is the way it is with those who turn again to their sin.

Psalm 103:12 He has removed our sins as far away from us as the east is from the west.

Romans 6:12 Do not let sin control your puny body any longer; do not give in to its sinful desires.

Romans 7:8–14 But sin used this law against evil desires by reminding me that such desires are wrong and arousing all kinds of forbidden desires within me! Only if there were no laws to break would there be no sinning.
  That is why I felt fine so long as I did not understand what the law really demanded. But when I learned the truth, I realized that I had broken the law and was a sinner, doomed to die. So as far as I was concerned, the good law which was supposed to show me the way of life resulted instead in my being given the death penalty. Sin fooled me by taking the good laws of God and using them to make me guilty of death. But still, you see, the law itself was wholly right and good.
  But how can that be? Didn't the law cause my downfall? How then can it be good? No, it was sin, devilish stuff that it is, that

used what was good to bring about my condemnation. So you can see how cunning and deadly and damnable it is. For it uses God's good laws for its own evil purposes. The law is good, then, and the trouble is not there but with *me*, because I am sold into slavery with sin as my owner.

1 John 1:8, 9a If we say that we have no sin, we are only fooling ourselves, and refusing to accept the truth. But if we confess our sins to him, he can be depended on to forgive us and to cleanse us from every wrong.

Proverbs 14:34 Godliness exalts a nation, but sin is a reproach to any people.

Proverbs 16:29 Wickedness loves company—and leads others into sin.

Psalm 36:1, 2 Sin lurks deep in the hearts of the wicked, forever urging them on to evil deeds. They have no fear of God to hold them back. Instead, in their conceit, they think they can hide their evil deeds and not get caught.

Psalm 32:1 What happiness for those whose guilt has been forgiven! What joys when sins are covered over! What relief for those who have confessed their sins and God has cleared their record.

Psalm 34:18 The Lord is close to those whose hearts are breaking, he rescues those who are humbly sorry for their sins.

1 John 3:9 The person who has been born into God's family does not make a practice of sinning, because now God's life is in him; so he can't keep on sinning, for this new life has been born into him and controls him—he has been *born again*.

1 Corinthians 8:12 And it is a sin against Christ to sin against your brother by encouraging him to do something he thinks is wrong.

Romans 8:2 For the power of the life-giving Spirit—and this power is mine through Christ Jesus—has freed me from the vicious circle of sin and death.

Proverbs 21:4   Pride, lust, and evil actions are all sin.

SORROW

Psalm 31:9, 10   O Lord, have mercy on me in my anguish. My eyes are red from weeping; my health is broken from sorrow. I am pining away with grief; my years are shortened, drained away because of sadness. My sins have sapped my strength; I stoop with sorrow and with shame.

2 Corinthians 7:10   For God sometimes uses sorrow in our lives to help us turn away from sin and seek eternal life. We should never regret his sending it. But the sorrow of the man who is not a Christian is not the sorrow of true repentance and does not prevent eternal death.

SUFFERING

Matthew 17:12b   And I, the Son of Mankind, shall also suffer at their hands.

Mark 8:31   Then he began to tell them about the terrible things he would suffer, and that he would be rejected by the elders and Chief Priests and the other Jewish leaders—and be killed, and that he would rise again three days afterwards.

John 16:33b   Here on earth you will have many trials and sorrows; but take courage, I have overcome the world.

Romans 8:17   And since we are his children, we will share his treasures—for all God gives to his Son Jesus is now ours too. But if we are to share his glory, we must also share his suffering.

2 Corinthians 12:7–10 . . . because these experiences I had were so tremendous, God was afraid I might be puffed up by them; so I was given a sickness which has been a thorn in my flesh, a messenger from Satan to hurt and bother me, and prick my pride. Three different times I begged God to make me well again. Each time he said, "No. But I am with you; that is all you need. My power shows up best in weak people." Now I am glad to boast about how weak I am; I am glad to be a living demonstration of Christ's power and abilities. Since I know it is all for Christ's good, I am quite happy about "the thorn", and about insults and hardships, persecutions and difficulties; for when I am weak, then I am strong—the less I have, the more I depend on him.

2 Timothy 2:12 And if we think that our present service for him is hard, just remember that some day we are going to sit with him and rule with him. But if we give up when we suffer, and turn against Christ, then he must turn against us.

Hebrews 5:8 Even though Jesus was God's Son, he had to learn from experience what it was like to obey, when obeying meant suffering.

1 Peter 2:20–23 . . . If you do right and suffer for it, and are patient beneath the blows, God is well pleased. This suffering is all part of the work God has given you. Christ, who suffered for you, is your example . . . when he suffered, he did not threaten to get even; he left his case in the hands of God who always judges fairly.

TALENTS

Exodus 35:35–36:1   God has filled them . . . with unusual skills as jewellers, carpenters, embroidery designers . . . All the other craftsmen with God-given abilities are to assist . . . in constructing and furnishing the Tabernacle.

Romans 1:15   To the fullest extent of my ability, I am ready to come . . .

Romans 12:6–8   God has given each of us the ability to do certain things well. So if God has given you the ability to prophesy, then prophesy whenever you can—as often as your faith is strong enough to receive a message from God. If your gift is that of serving others, serve them well. If you are a teacher, do a good job of teaching. If you are a preacher, see to it that your sermons are encouraging and helpful. If God has given you money, be generous in helping others with it. If God has given you administrative ability and put you in charge of the work of others, take the responsibility seriously.

Read the whole of *1 Corinthians 12.*

Ephesians 4:7, 12   Christ has given each of us special abilities—whatever he wants us to have out of his rich storehouse of gifts. Why is it that he gives us these special abilities to do certain things best? It is that God's people will be equipped to do better work for him, building up the church, the body of Christ, to a position of strength and maturity.

1 Timothy 4:14, 15   Be sure to use the abilities God has given you . . . Put these abilities to work; throw yourself into your tasks so that everyone may notice your improvement and progress.

1 Peter 4:10   God has given each of you some special abilities; be sure to use them to help each other, passing on to others God's many kinds of blessings.

TALKING

Psalm 19:14   May my spoken words and unspoken thoughts be pleasing even to you, O Lord my Rock and my Redeemer.

Ecclesiastes 5:2, 5   Don't be a fool who doesn't even realize it is sinful to make rash promises to God, for he is in heaven and you are only here on earth, so let your words be few . . . It is far better not to say you'll do something than to say you will and then not do it.

Ecclesiastes 3:7b   . . . . A time to be quiet; A time to speak up.

Matthew 12:34b–37   ". . . A man's heart determines his speech. A good man's speech reveals the rich treasures within him. An evil-hearted man is filled with venom, and his speech reveals it. And I tell you this, that you must give account on Judgment Day for every idle word you speak. Your words now reflect your fate then: either you will be justified by them or you will be condemned."

Philemon 2:14, 15b, 16   In everything you do, stay away from complaining and arguing, so that no one can speak a word of blame against you . . . shine out among them like beacon lights, holding out to them the Word of Life.

James 3:2, 10   If anyone can control his tongue, it proves that he has perfect control over himself in every other way . . . Blessing and cursing come pouring out of the same mouth. Dear brothers, surely this is not right!

1 John 3:18   Little children, let us stop just SAYING we love people; let us REALLY love them, and show it by our actions.

Colossians 3:17   And whatever you do or say, let it be as a representative of the Lord Jesus, and come with him into the presence of God the Father to give him your thanks.

Matthew 10:19, 20 ". . . don't worry about what to say at your trial, for you will be given the right words at the right time. For it won't be you doing the talking—it will be the Spirit of your heavenly Father speaking through you!"

TEMPTATION

1 Corinthians 10:13 But remember this—the wrong desires that come into your life aren't anything new and different. Many others have faced exactly the same problems before you. And no temptation is irresistible. You can trust God to keep the temptation from becoming so strong that you can't stand up against it, for he has promised this and will do what he says. He will show you how to escape temptation's power so that you can bear up patiently against it.

Hebrews 2:18 For since he himself has now been through suffering and temptation, he knows what it is like when we suffer and are tempted, and he is wonderfully able to help us.

James 1:12, 13, 14, 15a Happy is the man who doesn't give in and do wrong when he is tempted, for afterwards he will get as his reward the crown of life that God has promised those who love him. And remember, when someone wants to do wrong it is never God who is tempting him, for God never wants to do wrong and never tempts anyone else to do it. Temptation is the pull of man's own evil thoughts and wishes. These evil thoughts lead to evil actions.

1 John 2:15, 16 Stop loving this evil world and all that it offers you, for when you love these things you show that you do not really love God; for all these worldly things, these evil desires—the craze for sex, the ambition to buy everything that appeals to you, and the pride that comes from wealth and importance—these are not from God. They are from this evil world itself.

Matthew 18:7, 8   Temptation to do wrong is inevitable, but woe to the man who does the tempting. So if your hand or foot causes you to sin, cut it off and throw it away. Better to enter heaven crippled than to be in hell with both of your hands and feet.

TIME

Ecclesiastes 3:1, 11   There is a right time for everything . . . everything is appropriate in its own time. But though God has planted eternity in the hearts of men, even so, man cannot see the whole scope of God's work from beginning to end.

Isaiah 60:22b   . . . I, the Lord, will bring it all to pass when it is time.

Psalm 31:14   You alone are my God; my times are in your hands.

Psalm 37:7, 34   Rest in the Lord; wait patiently for him to act . . . Don't be impatient for the Lord to act! Keep travelling steadily along his pathway and in due season he will honour you with every blessing . . .

Psalm 90:4–6   A thousand years are but as yesterday to you! They are like a single hour! We glide along the tides of time as swiftly as a racing river, and vanish as quickly as a dream. We are like grass that is green in the morning but mowed down and withered before evening shadows fall.

Psalm 90:12   Teach us to number our days and recognize how few they are; help us to spend them as we should.

Matthew 6:34   So don't be anxious about tomorrow. God will take care of your tomorrow too. Live one day at a time.

John 9:4   All of us must quickly carry out the tasks assigned us by the one who sent me, for there is little time left before the night falls and all work comes to an end.

Romans 13:11   Another reason for right living is this: you know how late it is; time is running out. Wake up, for the coming of the Lord is nearer now than when we first believed.

Matthew 25:13   So stay awake and be prepared, for you do not know the date or moment of my return.

Luke 12:40   So be ready all the time. For I, the Man of glory, will come when least expected.

1 Timothy 4:7   Don't waste time arguing over foolish ideas and silly myths and legends. Spend your time and energy in the exercise of keeping spiritually fit.

TRUTH

2 Samuel 7:28   For you are indeed God, and your words are truth.

Psalm 12:6   The Lord's promise is sure. He speaks no careless word; all he says is purest truth, like silver seven times refined.

Proverbs 12:19   Truth stands the test of time; lies are soon exposed.

Luke 21:33   Though all heaven and earth shall pass away, yet my words remain forever true.

John 7:28   Jesus called out . . . "You know me and where I was born and brought up, but I am the representative of one you don't know, and he is Truth."

John 8:32   ". . . you will know the truth, and the truth will set you free."

John 12:48   All who reject me and my message will be judged at the Day of Judgment by the truths I (Jesus) have spoken.

John 14:6   Jesus told Him, "I am the Way—yes, and the Truth and the Life."

John 16:13a   When the Holy Spirit, who is truth, comes, he will guide you into all truth.

John 18:37   Jesus said ". . . I came to bring truth to the world. All who love the truth are my followers."

Romans 3:4b   God's words will always prove true and right, no matter who questions them.

2 Corinthians 5:7   We know these things are true by believing, not by seeing.

2 Timothy 3:16   Every Scripture was given to us by inspiration from God and is invaluable to teach us what is true and to make us realize what is wrong in our lives.

2 Timothy 2:19   God's truth stands firm like a great rock, and nothing can shake it.

WISDOM

Proverbs 1:7, 8   How does a man become wise? The first step is to trust and reverence the Lord!

Only fools refuse to be taught.

Proverbs 2:6, 9, 10   For the Lord grants wisdom! His every word is a treasure of knowledge and understanding. He shows how to distinguish right from wrong, how to find the right decision every time. For wisdom and truth will enter the very centre of your being, filling your life with joy.

Proverbs 8:12, 13   Wisdom and good judgment live together, for wisdom knows where to discover knowledge and understanding. If anyone respects and fears God, he will hate evil. For wisdom hates pride, arrogance, corruption and deceit of every kind.

Proverbs 14:33   Wisdom is enshrined in the hearts of men of common sense, but it must shout loudly before fools will hear it.

Psalm 16:7   I will bless the Lord who counsels me; he gives me wisdom in the night. He tells me what to do.

WORK

Proverbs 14:23   Work brings profit; talk brings poverty.

Proverbs 12:9, 11   It is better to get your hands dirty—and eat, than to be too proud to work—and starve.
   Hard work means prosperity; only a fool idles away his time.

Proverbs 21:25, 26   The lazy man longs for many things but his hands refuse to work. He is greedy to get, while the godly love to give!

Ephesians 6:6, 7   Don't work hard only when your master is watching and then shirk when he isn't looking; work hard and with gladness all the time, as though working for Christ, doing the will of God with all your hearts.

2 Thessalonians 3:10b   "He who does not work shall not eat."

MĒTI TELEĪ

This book is not finished! That is your privilege. As you study God's Word you will discover Scripture to add to these pages.

"May God who gives patience, steadiness, and encouragement help you to live in complete harmony with each other— each with the attitude of Christ towards the other."

"And he is able to keep you from slipping and falling away and to bring you, sinless and perfect, into his glorious presence with mighty shouts of everlasting joy."

HALLELUJAH!